ZIML Math Competition Book

Division H 2018-2019

Areteem Institute

ZIML Math Competition Book Division H 2018-2019

Edited by   John Lensmire
            David Reynoso
            Kevin Wang
            Kelly Ren

Copyright © 2019 ARETEEM INSTITUTE
WWW.ARETEEM.ORG

PUBLISHED BY ARETEEM PRESS
ALL RIGHTS RESERVED. No part of this publication may be reproduced, stored in a retrieval system, or transmitted, in any form or by any means, electronic, mechanical, photocopying, recording, or otherwise, without prior written permission of the publisher, except for "fair use" or other noncommercial uses as defined in Sections 107 and 108 of the U.S. Copyright Act.

ISBN-10: 1-944863-46-X
ISBN-13: 978-1-944863-46-3

First printing, August 2019.

TITLES PUBLISHED BY ARETEEM PRESS

Cracking the High School Math Competitions (and Solutions Manual) - Covering AMC 10 & 12, ARML, and ZIML

Mathematical Wisdom in Everyday Life (and Solutions Manual) - From Common Core to Math Competitions

Geometry Problem Solving for Middle School (and Solutions Manual) - From Common Core to Math Competitions

Fun Math Problem Solving For Elementary School (and Solutions Manual)

ZIML MATH COMPETITION BOOK SERIES

ZIML Math Competition Book Division E 2016-2017
ZIML Math Competition Book Division M 2016-2017
ZIML Math Competition Book Division H 2016-2017
ZIML Math Competition Book Jr Varsity 2016-2017
ZIML Math Competition Book Varsity Division 2016-2017
ZIML Math Competition Book Division E 2017-2018
ZIML Math Competition Book Division M 2017-2018
ZIML Math Competition Book Division H 2017-2018
ZIML Math Competition Book Jr Varsity 2017-2018
ZIML Math Competition Book Varsity Division 2017-2018
ZIML Math Competition Book Division E 2018-2019
ZIML Math Competition Book Division M 2018-2019
ZIML Math Competition Book Division H 2018-2019
ZIML Math Competition Book Jr Varsity 2018-2019
ZIML Math Competition Book Varsity Division 2018-2019

MATH CHALLENGE CURRICULUM TEXTBOOKS SERIES

Math Challenge I-A Pre-Algebra and Word Problems
Math Challenge I-B Pre-Algebra and Word Problems
Math Challenge I-C Algebra
Math Challenge II-A Algebra
Math Challenge II-B Algebra
Math Challenge III Algebra

Math Challenge I-A Geometry
Math Challenge I-B Geometry
Math Challenge I-C Topics in Algebra
Math Challenge II-A Geometry
Math Challenge II-B Geometry
Math Challenge III Geometry
Math Challenge I-A Counting and Probability
Math Challenge I-B Counting and Probability
Math Challenge I-C Geometry
Math Challenge II-A Combinatorics
Math Challenge II-B Combinatorics
Math Challenge III Combinatorics
Math Challenge I-A Number Theory
Math Challenge I-B Number Theory
Math Challenge I-C Finite Math
Math Challenge II-A Number Theory
Math Challenge II-B Number Theory
Math Challenge III Number Theory

COMING SOON FROM ARETEEM PRESS

Fun Math Problem Solving For Elementary School Vol. 2 (and Solutions Manual)
Counting & Probability for Middle School (and Solutions Manual) - From Common Core to Math Competitions
Number Theory Problem Solving for Middle School (and Solutions Manual) - From Common Core to Math Competitions

The books are available in paperback and eBook formats (including Kindle and other formats).
To order the books, visit https://areteem.org/bookstore.

Contents

Introduction 7

1   ZIML Contests 15
1.1   October 2018 17
1.2   November 2018 25
1.3   December 2018 33
1.4   January 2019 41
1.5   February 2019 47
1.6   March 2019 55
1.7   April 2019 63
1.8   May 2019 73
1.9   June 2019 81

2   ZIML Solutions 89
2.1   October 2018 90
2.2   November 2018 99
2.3   December 2018 109
2.4   January 2019 120
2.5   February 2019 132

Copyright © ARETEEM INSTITUTE. All rights reserved.

2.6	March 2019	144
2.7	April 2019	156
2.8	May 2019	170
2.9	June 2019	184
3	**Appendix**	**197**
3.1	Division H Topics Covered	197
3.2	Glossary of Common Math Terms	201
3.3	ZIML Answers	210

Introduction

Each month during the school year, Areteem Institute hosts the online Zoom International Math League (ZIML) competitions. Students can compete in one of five divisions based on their age and mathematical level (details shown on Page 9).

This book contains the problems, answers, and full solutions from the nine ZIML Division H Competitions held during the 2018-2019 School Year. It is divided into three parts:

1. The complete Division H ZIML Competitions (20 questions per competition) from October 2018 to June 2019.
2. The solutions for each of the competitions, including detailed work and helpful tricks.
3. An appendix including the topics and knowledge points covered for Division H, a glossary including common mathematical terms, and answer keys for each of the competitions so students can easily check their work.

The questions found on the ZIML competitions are meant to test your problem solving skills and train you to apply the knowledge you know to many different applications. We hope you enjoy the problems!

Copyright © ARETEEM INSTITUTE. All rights reserved.

About Zoom International Math League

The Zoom International Math League (ZIML) has a simple goal: provide a platform for students to build and share their passion for math and other STEM fields with students from around the globe. Started in 2008 as the Southern California Mathematical Olympiad, ZIML has a rich history of past participants who have advanced to top tier colleges and prestigious math competitions, including American Math Competitions, MATHCOUNTS, and the International Math Olympaid.

The ZIML Core Online Programs, most available with a free account at ziml.areteem.org, include:

- **Daily Magic Spells:** Provides a problem a day (Monday through Friday) for students to practice, with full solutions available the next day.
- **Weekly Brain Potions:** Provides one problem per week posted in the online discussion forum at ziml.areteem.org. Usually the problem does not have a simple answer, and students can join the discussion to share their thoughts regarding the scenarios described in the problem, explore the math concepts behind the problem, give solutions, and also ask further questions.
- **Monthly Contests:** The ZIML Monthly Contests are held the first weekend of each month during the school year (October through June). Students can compete in one of 5 divisions to test their knowledge and determine their strengths and weaknesses, with winners announced after the competition.
- **Math Competition Practice:** The Practice page contains sample ZIML contests and an archive of AMC-series tests for online practice. The practices simulate the real contest environment with time-limits of the contests automatically controlled by the server.
- **Online Discussion Forum:** The Online Discussion Forum

is open for any comments and questions. Other discussions, such as hard Daily Magic Spells or the Weekly Brain Potions are also posted here.

These programs encourage students to participate consistently, so they can track their progress and improvement each year.

In addition to the online programs, ZIML also hosts onsite Local Tournaments and Workshops in various locations in the United States. Each summer, there are onsite ZIML Competitions at held at Areteem Summer Programs, including the International ZIML Convention, which is a two day convention with one day of workshops and one day of competition.

ZIML Monthly Contests are organized into five divisions ranging from upper elementary school to advanced material based on high school math.

- **Varsity:** This is the top division. It covers material on the level of the last 10 questions on the AMC 12 and AIME level. This division is open to all age levels.
- **Junior Varsity:** This is the second highest competition division. It covers material at the AMC 10/12 level and State and National MathCounts level. This division is open to all age levels.
- **Division H:** This division focuses on material from a standard high school curriculum. It covers topics up to and including pre-calculus. This division will serve as excellent practice for students preparing for the math portions of the SAT or ACT. This division is open to all age levels.
- **Division M:** This division focuses on problem solving using math concepts from a standard middle school math curriculum. It covers material at the level of AMC 8 and School or Chapter MathCounts. This division is open to all students who have not started grade 9.

- **Division E:** This division focuses on advanced problem solving with mathematical concepts from upper elementary school. It covers material at a level comparable to MOEMS Division E. This division is open to all students who have not started grade 6.

This problem book features the Division H Contests. For a detailed list of topics covered for Division H see p.197 in the Appendix.

To participate in the ZIML Online Programs, create a free account at ziml.areteem.org. The ZIML site features are also provided on the ZIML Mobile App, which is available for download from Apple's App Store and Google Play Store.

Introduction

About Areteem Institute

Areteem Institute is an educational institution that develops and provides in-depth and advanced math and science programs for K-12 (Elementary School, Middle School, and High School) students and teachers. Areteem programs are accredited supplementary programs by the Western Association of Schools and Colleges (WASC). Students may attend the Areteem Institute in one or more of the following options:

- Live and real-time face-to-face online classes with audio, video, interactive online whiteboard, and text chatting capabilities;
- Self-paced classes by watching the recordings of the live classes;
- Short video courses for trending math, science, technology, engineering, English, and social studies topics;
- Summer Intensive Camps held on prestigious university campuses and Winter Boot Camps;
- Practice with selected free daily problems and monthly ZIML competitions at `ziml.areteem.org`.

Areteem courses are designed and developed by educational experts and industry professionals to bring real world applications into STEM education. The programs are ideal for students who wish to build their mathematical strength in order to excel academically and eventually win in Math Competitions (AMC, AIME, USAMO, IMO, ARML, MathCounts, Math Olympiad, ZIML, and other math leagues and tournaments, etc.), Science Fairs (County Science Fairs, State Science Fairs, national programs like Intel Science and Engineering Fair, etc.) and Science Olympiads, or for students who purely want to enrich their academic lives by taking more challenging courses and developing outstanding analytical, logical, and creative problem solving skills.

Since 2004 Areteem Institute has been teaching with methodology that is highly promoted by the new Common Core State Standards: stressing the conceptual level understanding of the math concepts, problem solving techniques, and solving problems with real world applications. With the guidance from experienced and passionate professors, students are motivated to explore concepts deeper by identifying an interesting problem, researching it, analyzing it, and using a critical thinking approach to come up with multiple solutions.

Thousands of math students who have been trained at Areteem have achieved top honors and earned top awards in major national and international math competitions, including Gold Medalists in the International Math Olympiad (IMO), top winners and qualifiers at the USA Math Olympiad (USAMO/JMO) and AIME, top winners at the Zoom International Math League (ZIML), and top winners at the MathCounts National Competition. Many Areteem Alumni have graduated from high school and gone on to enter their dream colleges such as MIT, Cal Tech, Harvard, Stanford, Yale, Princeton, U Penn, Harvey Mudd College, UC Berkeley, or UCLA. Those who have graduated from colleges are now playing important roles in their fields of endeavor.

Further information about Areteem Institute, as well as updates and errata of this book, can be found online at `http://www.areteem.org`.

Introduction

Acknowledgments

This book contains the Online ZIML Division H Problems from the 2018-19 school year. These problems were created and compiled by the staff of Areteem Institute. These problems were inspired by questions from the Areteem Math Challenge Courses, past questions on the ACT/SAT/GRE, past math competitions, math textbooks, and countless other resources and people encountered by the Areteem Curriculum Department in their life devoted to math. We thank all these sources for growing and nurturing our passion for math.

The Areteem staff, including John Lensmire, David Reynoso, Kevin Wang, and Kelly Ren, are the main contributors who compiled, edited, and reviewed this book.

Lastly, thanks to all the students who have participated and continue to participate in the Zoom International Math League. Your dedication to the Daily Magic Spells and Monthly Contests makes all of this possible, and we hope you continue to enjoy ZIML for years to come!

1. ZIML Contests

This part of the book contains the Division H ZIML Contests from the 2018-19 School Year. There were nine monthly competitions, held on the dates found below:

- October 5-7
- November 2-4
- December 7-9
- January 4-6
- February 1-3
- March 1-3
- April 5-7
- May 3-5
- June 7-9

1.1 ZIML October 2018 Division H

Below are the 20 Problems from the Division H ZIML Competition held in October 2018.
The answer key is available on p.210 in the Appendix.
Full solutions to these questions are available starting on p.90.

Problem 1
Barry and Cary were solving quadratic equations. Barry solved the equation $2x^2 - 4x + 1 = 0$ while Cary solved the equation $x^2 - 4x + 2 = 0$. Barry took his largest answer and divided it by Cary's largest answer. What was the result, rounded to the nearest tenth?

Problem 2
Today Mr. Lang's class will be taking a class photo. There are 10 girls and 5 boys in his class. He will let his students decide where to stand in the photo, but will decide the arrangement of boys and girls. (For example, 2 girls then 1 boy then 2 girls etc.)

If Mr. Lang wants to arrange the photo so no two boys are standing next to each other, how many ways can he do so?

Problem 3
Farmer Jane's farmhouse is in the middle of her land. She has one rectangular field to her east and one to her west, both with the same area. The eastern field is 700 yards longer than it is wide. The western field is 400 yards wide and 450 yards shorter than the first. Jane needs to build a fence around both fields. How many yards of fence does she need?

Problem 4
The graphs $y = mx$ and $y = 4\sqrt{x} - 1$ intersect at a point (or points) where $y \geq 0$. For how many integer m is this possible?

Problem 5
Consider the geometric sequence with recursive formula $a_0 = 12$ and $a_{n+1} = 18 \cdot a_n$. How many of the terms $a_0, a_1, \ldots, a_{99}$ are perfect cubes?

Problem 6
In $\triangle ABC$ denote the sides $AB = c$, $AC = b$, $BC = a$. Suppose $\angle C = 15°$ and the ratio $\dfrac{\angle A}{\angle B} = \dfrac{8}{3}$. The ratio $\dfrac{a^2}{b^2}$ can be written as $\dfrac{N}{M}$ for positive integers N, M with $\gcd(N, M) = 1$. What is $N + M$?

Problem 7
Solve the equation $\log_4(x^2) + \log_2(x) + \log_{1/2}(x) = 4$ over the real numbers. What is the smallest solution x, rounded to the nearest integer?

Problem 8
Peter is attending his friend's wedding next month. Peter has 3 dress shirts he can wear, 3 pairs of pants, and 2 different pairs of shoes. He needs to pick what to wear (one shirt, one pair of pants, and one pair of shoes) for both the ceremony and the reception afterwards. He may wear the same piece of clothing twice, but does not want to dress exactly the same for the ceremony and reception. How many choices does Peter have for what to wear?

Problem 9
Consider the equation $4\sin^2(x) + 2\sin(2x) = 0$. How many solutions are there such that $0° \le x \le 1000°$?

Problem 10

For this question, use $\dfrac{1.7 \cdot s^2}{4}$ to approximate the area of an equilateral triangle with side length s.

The labeled cube below has sides of length 2. Cut through vertices A, C, and F to form a triangular pyramid with vertices A, B, C, and F.

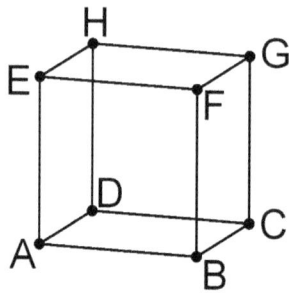

What is the surface area of this pyramid, rounded to the nearest tenth?

Problem 11

The five-digit number $\overline{12A4B}$ is divisible by 45. If all five digits are distinct, what is this number?

Problem 12

Consider the polynomial remainder when $x^4 + 2x^2 + 3x + 4$ is divided by $x^2 - 3$. This remainder has one zero in the form $\dfrac{P}{Q}$ for integers P, Q with $\gcd(P, Q) = 1$ and $Q > 0$. What is $Q - P$?

1.1 ZIML October 2018 Division H

Problem 13
Let point O denote the origin. Point A is on the line $y = 2x$ with the perpendicular bisector of $\overline{OA}$ intersecting the x-axis at $(7.5, 0)$. What is the y-value of A? Round your answer to the nearest tenth.

Problem 14
N is a positive integer such that $\gcd(N, 504) = 14$ and $\operatorname{lcm}(N, 84) = 420$. What is N?

Problem 15
After taking off right next to him at the park, Fred's drone flew a total distance of 200 meters with an angle of elevation of $30°$ traveling north. (Recall the angle of elevation is the angle the drone's path makes with the ground.)

The drone then traveled west for 400 meters, no longer changing it's elevation, and began to hover. The drone's distance from Fred in meters can be written as $\sqrt{K}$ for an integer K. What is K?

Problem 16

A baseball field is shown below, with distances measured in feet.

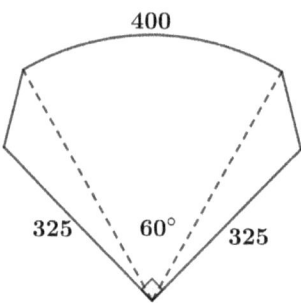

(Here all the sides are straight lines, except for the top, which is a circular arc with radius 400 ft.) Using the approximations $\pi \approx 3$ and $\sin(15°) \approx 0.25$, find the area of the baseball field, rounded to the nearest square foot.

Problem 17

The numbers $\sqrt{5}$ and $1+i$ are both solutions to the polynomial equation $x^4 + Bx^3 + Cx^2 + Dx - 10 = 0$. If B, C, and D are all integers, what is C? (Here $i = \sqrt{-1}$.)

Problem 18

In the circle shown below, lines $\overline{AD}$ and $\overline{BC}$ are parallel, with arc $\widehat{DE} = 30°$. The angles of $x°$ and $3x°$ are both integers.

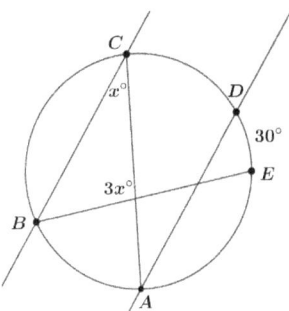

What is the value of x?

Problem 19

Sierra and Terry each roll a die. Sierra rolls a fair six-sided die labeled with the numbers 1 to 6 while Terry rolls a fair ten-sided die labeled with the numbers 1 to 10. The probability Terry's roll is larger than Sierra's can be written as $\dfrac{A}{B}$ for positive integers A and B with $\gcd(A,B) = 1$. What is $B - A$?

Problem 20

Two complex numbers p and q have product -4 and $p - q = 2$. p can be expressed as $A + i\sqrt{B}$ for positive integers A and B. What is $A + B$?

1.2 ZIML November 2018 Division H

Below are the 20 Problems from the Division H ZIML Competition held in November 2018.
The answer key is available on p.211 in the Appendix.
Full solutions to these questions are available starting on p.99.

Problem 1
Exactly one of the solutions to the equation

$$4+x+\frac{1}{x} = 4x+\frac{1}{4x}$$

can be written as $\frac{P}{Q}$ for positive integers P and Q with $\gcd(P,Q) = 1$. What is $P+Q$?

Problem 2
Bob and Tom were partners in geometry class. They were asked to find the angles in a regular polygon with n sides. One of them calculated the measure of one internal angle while the other found the angle of one external angle. Their results differed by $164°$. What is n?

Problem 3
Carrie rolls a fair six-sided die, with sides numbered 1 through 6. If the result is ≤ 4 she flips a fair coin twice. If the result is > 4 she flips a fair coin 3 times. The probability that Carrie gets at least one heads during the coin flips can be expressed as $\frac{P}{Q}$ for positive integers P and Q with $\gcd(P,Q) = 1$. What is $P+Q$?

Problem 4
Patrick was exploring the function $f(x) = \sqrt{x^2 - 18x + 98}$. He wrote a computer program to list out the values of

$$f(0), f(1), f(2), f(3)\ldots$$

except removing all decimals from the answer. For example, the first two outputs were both 9 because

$$f(0) = \sqrt{98} \approx 9.899 \text{ and } f(1) = \sqrt{81} = 9.$$

What integer will be the smallest output by Patrick's program?

Problem 5
Start with $\triangle ABC$. Draw a median AD of $\triangle ABC$ and then a median DE of $\triangle ADC$. Connect BE and draw a median EF of $\triangle BED$. Then the ratio of areas of $\triangle DEF$ to $\triangle ABC$, can be written $[DEF] : [ABC] = P : Q$ for positive integers P and Q with $\gcd(P, Q) = 1$. What is $P + Q$?

Problem 6
How many factors does the number 43560 have?

1.2 ZIML November 2018 Division H

Problem 7
Dylan is carving a pumpkin for Halloween. For this problem we assume the pumpkin has the shape of a sphere, and when Dylan removes the interior of the pumpkin (to make it hollow before carving) he also is removing a perfect sphere.

Dylan carves out the pumpkin so that the remaining pumpkin has a thickness of 2 inches. If Dylan removes approximately 166.67π cubic inches from the interior of the pumpkin, then the volume of the remaining pumpkin can be approximated as $P\pi$ where P is rounded to the nearest hundredth. What is P?

Problem 8
Two chords AB and CD are extended to intersect outside a circle as shown below.

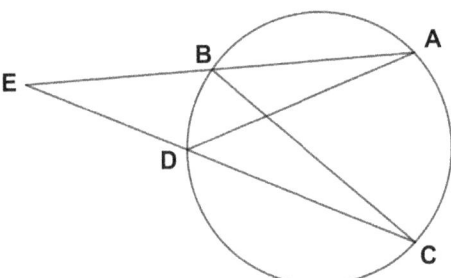

If $\angle AEC = 26°$ and chords AD and BC intersect at an acute angle of $62°$ what is the measure of arc $\widehat{AC}$? Round your answer to the nearest tenth.

Problem 9
Consider the product

$$\log_5(6) \cdot \log_6(7) \cdot \log_7(8) \cdots \log_{n-1}(n).$$

For how many integers $6 \leq n \leq 1000$ is this product an integer?

Problem 10
Don draws a pattern using unit squares. He starts with a 2×1 white rectangle, then he adds gray squares to form a 3×2 rectangle, then he adds white squares again to form a 4×3 rectangle, and continues in this manner. The first four rectangles are drawn below.

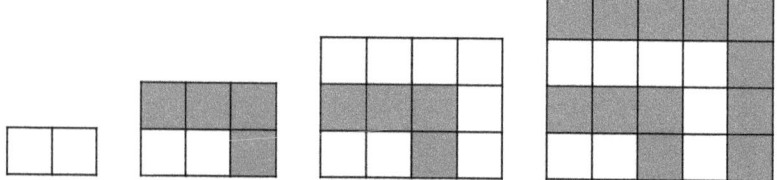

Consider the 11th rectangle in this pattern. How many white squares are there in this rectangle?

Problem 11
Find the product of all the integer solutions to the equation

$$|2x^2 - 29| = 21.$$

1.2 ZIML November 2018 Division H

Problem 12
Quadrilateral $ABCD$ with sides 6, 2, 4, and 4 is shown below, with $\angle A = 60°$ and $\angle C = 120°$.

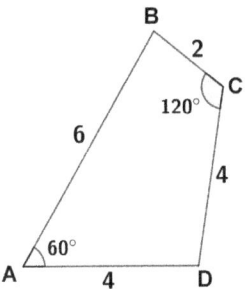

The area of $ABCD$ can be expressed as $\sqrt{M}$ for an integer M. What is M?

Problem 13
Jared lists all the perfect squares from one to ten thousand: $1, 4, 9, \ldots, 10000$. How many of these numbers are also multiples of 18?

Problem 14
The function $f(x) = x^3 + 2x + 4$ is always increasing, so it has an inverse function $f^{-1}(x)$. $f^{-1}(1357)$ is an integer K. What is K?

Problem 15
A circle with center on the line $y = 12 - 3x$ is tangent to both the x-axis and the y-axis. This circle has an equation that can be expressed in the form
$$Ax^2 + By^2 + Cx + Dy + E = 0,$$
where A, B, C, D, and E are all integers. What is $A + B + C + D + E$?

Problem 16
Recall that a complex number $a + bi$ can be plotted as the point (a, b) in the complex plane.

Start with $A = (1+i)$ and Let $B = A \cdot 2i$, $C = B \cdot 2i$, and $D = C \cdot 2i$. In the complex plane, $ABCD$ forms a quadrilateral. What is the area of this quadrilateral, rounded to the nearest integer?

Problem 17
Regular hexagon $ABCDEF$ has side length 6. Cut of triangles $\triangle ABF$ and $\triangle CDE$ to form quadrilateral $BCEF$. The area of $BCEF$ can be expressed as $R\sqrt{S}$ where R and S are positive integers with S having no square factors. What is $R + S$?

Problem 18
Monica got 8 candy bars, 5 caramel apples, and 6 packs of gum (19 different pieces of candy in total) for Halloween. She wants to pack 5 pieces of candy to take with her to her brother's soccer game. If the order of the candy she chooses does not matter and Monica brings exactly 2 candy bars, how many collections of candy can she bring to the game?

Problem 19
What is the units digit of

$$8^{31} + 1^{31} + 12^{31} + 12^{31} + 15^{31} + 23^{31} + 5^{31} + 5^{31} + 14^{31}?$$

Problem 20
Solve the equation

$$\tan(\theta)\tan(2\theta) + 3 = 0$$

for $0° \leq \theta < 360°$. What is the difference between the largest and smallest solution in this interval? Round your answer to the nearest degree.

1.3 ZIML December 2018 Division H

Below are the 20 Problems from the Division H ZIML Competition held in December 2018.
The answer key is available on p.212 in the Appendix.
Full solutions to these questions are available starting on p.109.

Problem 1
4 circles, each with radius 1, are arranged so that their centers form a square and opposite circles are tangent, as shown in the diagram below.

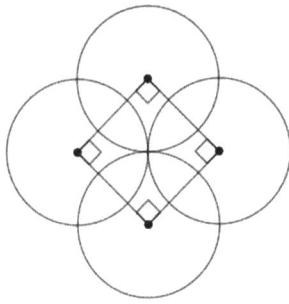

Consider the region made up of points contained inside at least one of the circles. Using the approximation $\pi \approx 3.14$, what is the area of this region?

Problem 2
The equation
$$x^6 - (2x)^3 = 2^7$$
has one integer solution. What is this solution?

Problem 3
Julie enjoys bird watching while she eats her breakfast. She knows she never sees more than 8 different birds and sometimes sees no birds at all.

Julie has recorded the birds she's seen this week in the table below:

Mon	Tue	Wed	Thu	Fri	Sat	Sun
3	1	7	0	5	?	?

After Julie completes the table she will calculate the median number of birds she has seen during the week. If L is the largest possible median and S is the smallest possible median, what is $L - S$?

Problem 4
Estimate the following. Round your final answer to the nearest integer.

$$\log_2(123) + \log_3(246) + \log_4(1023) + \log_5(3210)$$

Problem 5
$\triangle ABC$ is formed by the intersections of lines $y = \frac{1}{2}x$, $y = -2x$, and $y = 3$.

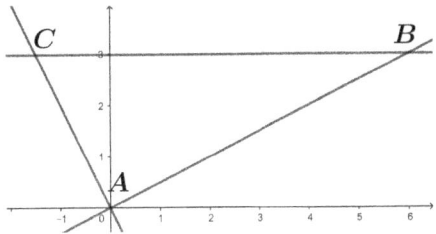

If D is the midpoint of $\overline{AB}$ and E is the midpoint of $\overline{AC}$, then the area of $\triangle BDE$ can be written as $\frac{P}{Q}$ for positive integers P and Q with $\gcd(P, Q) = 1$. What is $P + Q$?

Problem 6
How many of the integers $1, 2, 3, \ldots, 100$ are divisible by 5 or 7 but not both?

Problem 7

In Rick's Geometry class, he needed to find the equation of a circle. Rick gave an answer of

$$x^2 - 2x + y^2 + 4y = 4.$$

Rick's teacher said his answer was incorrect, but he would get the correct answer if he shifted the center of his circle up (vertically) +2 units and increased the radius by 2. With this hint, Rick got the correct answer of

$$x^2 + y^2 + Ax + By = C.$$

What is $A + B + C$?

Problem 8

Find the sum of all integer m such that the graphs of $y = x^2 + mx + 1$ and $y = mx^2 + m$ intersect at least once.

Problem 9

Your mom sends you to the store to buy 3 different boxes of cereal, 1 gallon of milk, and one candy bar each for you and your sister.

The store has 6 choices of cereal, 3 choices of milk, and 5 choices of candy bars. How many different collections of groceries for your mom can you buy?

Problem 10
Recall that a parabola can be defined as the collection of points that are equal distance to the focus (a point) and the directrix (a line).

The parabola with focus $(2,3)$ and directrix $y = -5$ can be written as $y = \frac{1}{16}(x^2 + Bx + C)$ for integers B and C. What is B?

Problem 11
A square right pyramid has a surface area of $121 + 121\sqrt{3}$. If all the edges of the pyramid have integer length N, what is N?

Problem 12
Find the last two digits of 2009^{2003}.

Problem 13
Simplify
$$2 - \cfrac{2}{2 - \cfrac{2}{2 - \cfrac{2}{2 - \cfrac{2}{2 - \cfrac{2}{1-i}}}}}$$
to $A + Bi$ where A and B are both integers. What is $A^2 + B^2$?

Problem 14
An octagon with 8 equal angles has sides of length 1, $\sqrt{2}$, and 2 as in the diagram below.

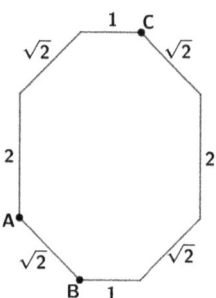

Calculate $\cos \angle ABC$ and write your answer in simplest radical form: $\dfrac{P\sqrt{Q}}{R}$ for integers P, Q, and R. What is $P+Q+R$?

Problem 15
Peter walks to school 20% of the time, rides his bike 50% of the time, and takes the school bus 30% of the time. He has a 50% chance of arriving on time for his first class if he walks, an 80% chance if he rides his bike, and a 90% chance if he takes the school bus. Overall Peter has a $K\%$ chance of arriving on time for his first class. What is K, rounded to the nearest integer?

Problem 16
In $\triangle ABC$, $AB = 5$ and $\sin \angle ACB = \dfrac{5}{7}$. Point D is on side $\overline{AC}$ such that $AD = 4$ and $\sin \angle ABD = \dfrac{4}{5}$. What is the length of BC? Round your answer to the nearest tenth.

Problem 17
Find the smallest $\theta > 180°$ such that $2\sin(2\theta + 30°) = \cos(2\theta) + \sqrt{3}$. Round your answer to the nearest degree if necessary. (Input just the number as your answer. For example, if $\theta = 181°$, input 181.)

Problem 18
Consider all the factors of 1000. The product of all these factors can be expressed as 10^K for an integer K. What is K?

Problem 19
Monica had a trapezoid flag on a stick as shown below.

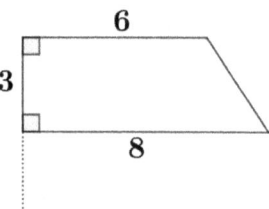

Monica rotates the flag around the stick, forming a three-dimensional solid. The volume of this solid can be written as $K \times \pi$ where K is an integer. What is K?

Problem 20
Two of the three roots of cubic polynomial $x^3 + Ax^2 + Bx + C = 0$ are 1 and $1 - i$. (Here A, B, and C are all integers.) What is C?

1.4 ZIML January 2019 Division H

Below are the 20 Problems from the Division H ZIML Competition held in January 2019.
The answer key is available on p.213 in the Appendix.
Full solutions to these questions are available starting on p.120.

Problem 1
In triangle $\triangle ABC$, $\angle C = 100°$. D is on AC so that $\overline{BD}$ bisects $\angle B$. If $\triangle ABD$ is isosceles, what is $\angle A$? Round your answer to the nearest tenth.

Problem 2
Claire's robotics club has 11 total members. This Friday, Saturday, and Sunday the club needs to members to volunteer at the local science fair. A group of two people is needed each day and no one will volunteer twice. How many different ways can the club decide the groups of volunteers for the three days?

Problem 3
Consider the prime factorization of $222,222$. What is the sum of all the distinct prime factors?

Problem 4
What is the x-intercept of the perpendicular bisector of line segment $\overline{AB}$ where $A = (-2,3)$ and $B = (4,6)$. Round your answer to the nearest hundredth if necessary.

Problem 5
Consider solutions to $|x^2+4x-2|=2$. What is the sum of the largest and smallest solutions? Round your answer to the nearest integer.

Problem 6
In a circle, the extensions of diameter $\overline{AB}$ and chord $\overline{CD}$ intersect at point E, as shown below.

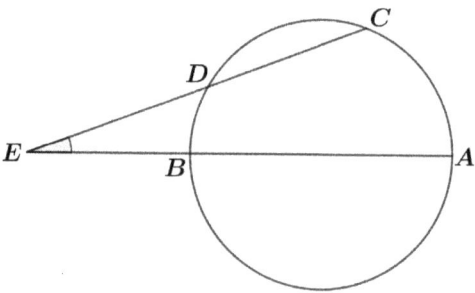

If $\angle AEC = 20°$ and minor arc $\widehat{CD}$ has measure $80°$, what is $\angle ABC$ in degrees? Round your answer to the nearest integer.

Problem 7
The equation
$$\sqrt{x^2+x+2}+x^2+x+2=6$$
has two integer roots A and B, with $A > B$. What is $A - B$?

Problem 8
In trapezoid $ABCD$, $AB \| CD$, $AB = 6$, and $CD = 9$. Diagonals $\overline{AC}$ and $\overline{BD}$ intersect at E and the area of $\triangle CDE$ is 27. What is the height of trapezoid $ABCD$? Round your answer to the nearest tenth.

Problem 9
In chess, a knight can move in an L shape (2 squares in one direction and 1 in another) as shown in the diagram below:

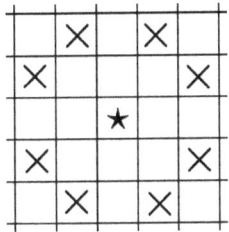

(A knight in the starred square ($\star$) can move to any of the squares with a cross ($\times$).)

How many ways can 2 identical knights be put on the 3×3 grid:

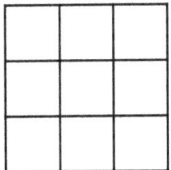

so that neither knight can move to the space occupied by the other?

Problem 10
A rectangular prism is cut by a plane into two pieces (both prisms) as shown below:

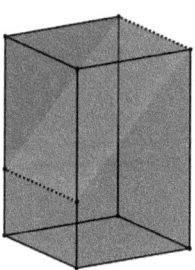

Then the ratio of the volumes of the two pieces can be written as $P:Q$ for positive integers $P<Q$ with $\gcd(P,Q)=1$. What is P^2+Q^2?

Problem 11
The distance from the vertex of parabola $y=x^2+6x+5$ to the vertex of $y=-x^2+10x-23$ can be written as $\sqrt{M}$ for an integer M. What is M?

Problem 12
Complex numbers $a \neq b$ are the two roots of a quadratic equation with rational coefficients.

If the sum of a and b is $\dfrac{4}{3}$ and the imaginary part of a is 3, then $a \times b$ can be written as $\dfrac{P}{Q}$ for integers P and Q with $Q>0$ and $\gcd(P,Q)=1$. What is $P+Q$?

1.4 ZIML January 2019 Division H

Problem 13
In triangle $\triangle ABC$, $AB = 2$ and $BC = 8$. Point D is on BC so that $AD = 4$ and $BD = 5$. AC^2 can be written as $\dfrac{P}{Q}$ for positive integers P and Q with $\gcd(P,Q) = 1$. What is $P+Q$?

Problem 14
The equation $\log_4(x) + \log_x(16) = \dfrac{9}{2}$ has two integer solutions. What is the sum of these solutions?

Problem 15
Triangle $\triangle ABC$ has sides $AB > BC$ with $BC = 6$ and angle $\angle B = 45°$. The area of the triangle is an integer K. What is the smallest possible value of K?

Problem 16
Eric and Morgan are going to the College Football Playoff National Championship. They are both flying into San Jose for the game. Suppose Eric's flight will arrive sometime randomly between 2 and 3 PM while Morgan's flight arrives sometime randomly between 2:30 PM and 4 PM.

The probability that Eric arrives after Morgan can be expressed as $K\%$. What is K, rounded to the nearest integer?

Problem 17
Recall $\lfloor x \rfloor$ is the greatest integer $\leq x$. For example, $\lfloor \sqrt{2} \rfloor = 1$ and $\lfloor -\pi \rfloor = -4$.

Define a recursive sequence as follows. $a_0 = 4$ and, for $n \geq 1$,

$$a_n = \lfloor (-1)^n \sqrt{(a_{n-1})^2 + 1} \rfloor$$

What is a_{20}?

Problem 18
The parabola $y = x^2 - 4$ and the circle $x^2 + y^2 = 4$ intersect at 4 points, determining a quadrilateral. The area of this quadrilateral can be written in simplest radical form as $A + B\sqrt{C}$ where A, B, and C are all positive integers with C having no square factors. What is $A + B + C$?

Problem 19
The seven-digit number $\overline{20ab1a9}$ is divisible by 99. What is $10a + b$?

Problem 20
Solve the equation

$$2\sin(2x) = \sqrt{3} \times \frac{\cos(4x)}{\cos(2x)}$$

for x in degrees. What is the sum of all such x with $0° < x < 180°$? Round your answer to the nearest degree.

1.5 ZIML February 2019 Division H

Below are the 20 Problems from the Division H ZIML Competition held in February 2019.
The answer key is available on p.214 in the Appendix.
Full solutions to these questions are available starting on p.132.

Problem 1
x, y, and z are real numbers satisfying

$$x + 2y + 3z = 9$$
$$x + 3y + 2z = 8$$
$$y + 2z = 5.$$

What is $x^2 + y^2 + z^2$? Round your answer to the nearest tenth.

Problem 2
Becky rolls a fair six-sided die (numbered $1-6$) three times and records the results of all three rolls. The probability that the first roll is greater than the sum of the second and third rolls can be written as $\dfrac{P}{Q}$ for positive integers P and Q with $\gcd(P,Q) = 1$. What is $Q - P$?

Problem 3
Find the last digit of $2^{100} + 19^{100}$.

Problem 4
Carrie took the 13 different hearts out of a standard deck of cards. This gave her 9 numbered cards $(2, 3, \ldots, 10)$ and 4 face cards $(J, Q, K,$ and $A)$. Carrie randomly dealt 5 cards out in a line and noticed that she had one face card and the other 4 (numbered cards) appeared in increasing order. How many different ways could Carrie have dealt out the cards?

Problem 5
Trapezoid $ABCD$ with $\overline{AB} \parallel \overline{CD}$ is shown below, with $CD = AE = EF = BF$.

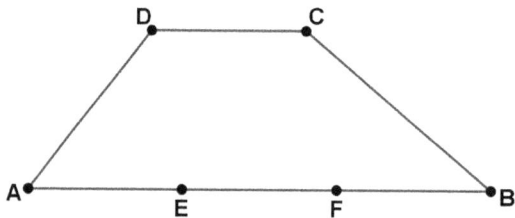

Let G be the intersection of $\overline{CE}$ and $\overline{DF}$. The area of pentagon $EFCGD$ is $K\%$ of the entire trapezoid. What is K, rounded to the nearest tenth?

Problem 6
A regular pentagon, regular hexagon, regular octagon, and regular decagon are drawn around a square as shown below.

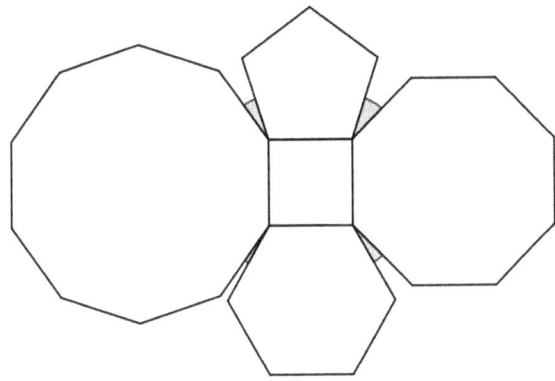

This creates four angles (in the gaps). What is the sum of these four angles in degrees?

Problem 7
Let c be the complex number $c = 1 + 2i$, where $i = \sqrt{-1}$. The imaginary part of the expression $c^2 + \dfrac{1}{c^2}$ can be written as $\dfrac{P}{Q}$ for integers P and Q with $Q > 0$ and $\gcd(P, Q) = 1$. What is $P + Q$?

Problem 8
The first four terms of a sequence are

$$1, i, i+1, i-1,$$

where we alternate multiplying by i and adding 1 after the first term. The hundredth term in this sequence can be expressed as $A + Bi$ for integers A and B. What is $2A + 3B$?

Recall $i = \sqrt{-1}$.

Problem 9
For how many integer values of k does $y = 2kx^2 + 8x + k$ have two real roots?

Problem 10
Consider the smallest perfect square integer N that is a multiple of 430848. How many factors does N have?

Problem 11
A right triangle has area 96. If its three sides form an arithmetic progression, what is the smallest side? Round your answer to the nearest integer.

Problem 12
Peter starts with a cube with side length 4 inches. In the center of each of the faces, he cuts out a 1 inch cube. What is the surface area (in square inches) of this solid?

Problem 13
The circle below has diameter 12.

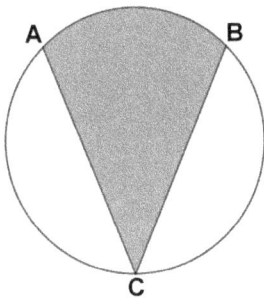

If the measure of $\widehat{AB}$ is $90°$ and $AC = BC$, the area of the shaded region can be written as $A\pi + B\sqrt{C}$ for integers A, B, and C with C containing no squares as factors. What is $A + B + C$?

Problem 14
Two circles, one with center $(3,0)$ and radius 5 and the other with center $(-7,5)$ and radius $5\sqrt{2}$ intersect at two points. The midpoint of these two points is (M,N). What is $M + N$? Round your answer to the nearest integer.

Problem 15
Consider the equation $x^4 - 9x^2 + 20 = 0$. What is the product of all the integer solutions to this equation?

Problem 16
Point A has coordinates $(3, 1)$. It is rotated $30°$ counterclockwise about the origin as shown below.

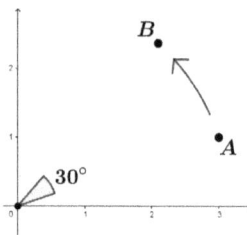

Let D denote the distance from A to B. Using the approximation $\sqrt{3} = 1.73$, what is D^2? Round your answer to the nearest tenth.

Problem 17
What is the smallest integer value of $L > 0$ such that $y = 2x$, $y = 4x$, $y = 6x$, and $y = 8x$ each intersect the line $y = L$ at integer values of x?

Problem 18
The minimum value of the quadratic $y = x^2 - 6x + 13$ is the same as the maximum value of the quadratic $y = -x^2 - 2x + P$? What is P? Round your answer to the nearest integer if necessary.

Problem 19
Solve the equation
$$\cos(x) \cdot \cos(2x) \cdot \cos(3x) \cdot \cos(4x) = 0.$$
What is the sum of all solutions with $0° \leq x < 180°$? Round your answer to the nearest tenth.

Problem 20
The inverse of $f(x)$ is given by the equation
$$f^{-1}(x) = \log_2(4x-1).$$
$f(3)$ can be written as $\dfrac{P}{Q}$ for integers P and $Q > 0$ with $\gcd(P,Q) = 1$. What is $P+Q$?

1.6 ZIML March 2019 Division H

Below are the 20 Problems from the Division H ZIML Competition held in March 2019.
The answer key is available on p.215 in the Appendix.
Full solutions to these questions are available starting on p.144.

Problem 1
Tracy solves the equation $\tan(\theta) = \sin(\theta)$.

Iggy solves the equation $\sin(\theta)\cos(\theta) = \sin(\theta)$.

They each write all the solutions they found with $0° \leq \theta < 360°$. How many solutions written by Tracy are also written by Iggy?

Problem 2
Three angles in a pentagon are congruent. The fourth angle measures $20°$ larger than these three angles. The fifth angle measures $80°$ less than the three congruent angles. What is the measure of one of the three congruent angles?

Problem 3
Stan has 5 different Guardians of the Galaxy action figures and 6 different Avengers action figures. How many ways can he arrange 3 of each (so 6 in total) in a line?

Problem 4
In the diagram below, the full shape is a square and each of the points shown are midpoints.

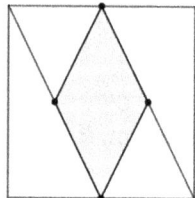

If the shaded region has area 16, what is the area of the full square?

Problem 5
Consider the graph of

$$y = -x + 4\sqrt{x} + 12.$$

This graph has a maximum value of $y = S$ achieved when $x = R$. What is $R + S$? Round your answer to the nearest integer.

Problem 6
In Ted's old arcade football game, you could either score 3 points (with a field goal) or 7 points (with a touchdown). For example, this means it was never possible to have a score of 8 points. How many different scores from 0 to 50 (including both 0 and 50) are possible?

1.6 ZIML March 2019 Division H

Problem 7
M and N are positive real numbers such that $\log(M) = 1.5$ and $\log(N) = -0.2$. Calculate

$$\log\left(\frac{100\sqrt{M^3}}{N^2}\right).$$

Round your answer to the nearest hundredth.

Here $\log(x)$ denotes the common logarithm of x.

Problem 8
$\triangle ABC$ has

$$\angle A = 30°, \angle C = 45°, AB = 5\sqrt{2}$$

and $\triangle DEF$ has

$$\angle D = 45°, \angle E = 105°, DE = 3.$$

Then the area of $\triangle ABC$ is R times the area of $\triangle DEF$. What is R, rounded to the nearest tenth?

Problem 9
Kevin was collecting data for a school project, where he asked a total of 84 Boys and Girls at his school whether they preferred red or yellow for their school colors. Unfortunately his dog ripped up some of his chart and he could only read the data shown below.

	Red	Yellow	Total
Boys	??	??	40
Girls	??	12	??
Total	??	30	84

If Kevin randomly asked one of the students who preferred red, the probability that they are a girl can be written as $\frac{P}{Q}$ for positive integers P and Q with $\gcd(P,Q) = 1$. What is $P+Q$?

Problem 10
Charles and Greg are growing pea plants. In week 0, Charles' plant starts at a height of 2 cm and grows 20% taller each week. Greg's plant starts at a height of 0.75 cm and grows 60% taller each week. If they measure the height each week, then week N is the first week that Greg's plant is taller than Charles'. What is N?

Problem 11
A transformation maps the point (x,y) to $(-2y,-2x)$ in the xy-plane. Let $\triangle A'B'C'$ be the image of $\triangle ABC$ under this transformation, with $A = (2,2)$, $B = (-2,0)$, and $C = (-5,2)$. What is the area of $\triangle A'B'C'$? Round your answer to the nearest integer.

Problem 12
Find the largest 6-digit number of the form $\overline{3A19B4}$ that is divisible by 44.

Problem 13
In a circle of diameter 4, chords $\overline{AB}$ and $\overline{CD}$ intersect at an angle of $\theta°$, with $\theta° < 90°$. If $AB = 4$, $AC = 2$, and $BD = 2\sqrt{2}$, what is θ, rounded to the nearest integer?

Problem 14
Consider powers of the complex number $1 + i\sqrt{3}$:

$$(1+i\sqrt{3}), (1+i\sqrt{3})^2, \ldots, (1+i\sqrt{3})^{100}.$$

How many of these first hundred powers are integers?

Here i denotes $\sqrt{-1}$.

Problem 15
M is the only positive integer that is a multiple of 45 and 200 that has exactly 45 factors. What is M?

Problem 16
For a unique positive integer a the function

$$f(x) = 4x^4 - (ax^2 + 3x + 2)^2$$

is a degree 3 polynomial. What is the leading coefficient of this polynomial?

Problem 17

Peter has a solid rubber ball with volume $\dfrac{32\pi}{3}$ cubic inches that fits nicely in a box he has with length and width 4 inches and a height of 3 inches. Keeping the ball fixed, he cuts off the top of the ball outside the box, as shown below.

This leaves a circle shape as the new top of the ball. The area of this circle can be written as $M\pi$ for a real number M. What is M, rounded to the nearest tenth?

Problem 18

On a standard, fair 6-sided die, the numbers 1 and 6 are red, while 2, 3, 4, and 5 are blue. If the die is rolled 5 times, the probability that exactly two of the rolls are red is $K\%$. What is K, rounded to the nearest integer?

Problem 19
Parabola 1 opens vertically with equation $y = ax^2 + bx + c$ while Parabola 2 opens horizontally with equation $x = dy^2 + ey + f$. Both parabolas have vertex $(2, -1)$ and intersect at the point $(3, 0)$. The distance between the y-intercept of Parabola 1 and the x-intercept of Parabola 2 can be written as $\sqrt{S}$ for an integer S. What is S?

Problem 20
Consider the two parabolas
$$y = x^2 + (k-2)x + (1-k)$$
$$y = x^2 - 8x + k^2.$$

For how many integers k do both parabolas have the same number of x-intercepts?

1.7 ZIML April 2019 Division H

Below are the 20 Problems from the Division H ZIML Competition held in April 2019.
The answer key is available on p.216 in the Appendix.
Full solutions to these questions are available starting on p.156.

Problem 1
Two circles of radius 2 are tangent at point C. A line ℓ is tangent to both circles, at points A and B. What is the perimeter of the region bounded by line segment $\overline{AB}$, arc $\widehat{AC}$, and arc $\widehat{BC}$? Round your answer to the nearest tenth.

Problem 2
The equation $(x+2)^4 = (x-2)^4$ has one nonzero complex root of the form $A + Bi$ were A and B are nonnegative real numbers. What is $A + B$?

Problem 3
What is the remainder when $4^{2019} + 6^{2019}$ is divided by 9?

Problem 4
Congruent copies of a pentagon are shown tiling a plane in the diagram below.

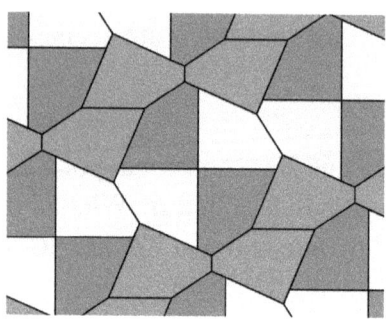

If the largest angle of the pentagon is 150°, what is the smallest angle? Round your answer to the nearest degree.

Note: The diagram above is not necessarily drawn to scale.

Problem 5
A parabola $y = ax^2 + bx + c$ with $a > 0$ contains the points $(-1, 1)$ and $(3, 5)$. Consider the parabola containing these points whose minimum (y-value) is as large as possible. For this parabola a can be written as $\dfrac{P}{Q}$ for positive integers P and Q with $\gcd(P, Q) = 1$. What is $P + Q$?

Problem 6
Tomorrow is picture day for the triplets Trenton, Tristan, and Troy. They'll be taking a photo with their science club, which consists of them and 5 other classmates. They've always wanted a photo where at least two of them stand together. Unfortunately the order the club lines up is completely random. How many ways can the club line up so that the triplets get their wish? (Do not assume all the triplets look identical for the photo.)

Problem 7
The function $f(x)$ has domain all real numbers $x > \dfrac{3}{2}$ with

$$f(x) = \frac{1}{(2x-3)^2} - \frac{3x+3}{2x^2-x-3}.$$

On this domain, there is one solution to $f(x) = 4$, which can be expressed as $\dfrac{P}{Q}$ for positive integers P and Q with $\gcd(P,Q) = 1$. What is $P + Q$?

Problem 8
What is the smallest positive value of θ (measured in degrees) with θ a solution to $|\sin(\theta)| = \cos(\theta)$ but not a solution to $\sin(\theta) = \cos(\theta)$? Round your answer to the nearest degree.

Problem 9
A square pyramid is formed by folding up the net below:

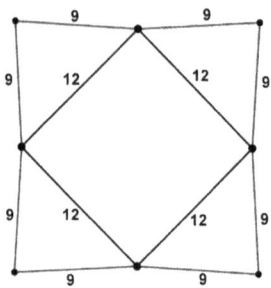

What is the volume of this pyramid?

Problem 10
Carrie is looking for 3-digit numbers $N = \overline{ABC}$ with the following properties: (i) N is a multiple of 10, (ii) N contains no perfect squares as factors, and (iii) $A + C - B = 0$. What is the sum of all possible N?

Problem 11
Manny's dad wants to build a fire pit in their backyard. He has blocks that are isosceles trapezoids with largest interior angle of 99°. He arranges them in a circle as shown below.

How many blocks does Manny's dad need to complete the fire pit?

Problem 12
Find the sum of all rational solutions to $3 \cdot 2^{x+2} = \dfrac{864}{3^{x-1}}$. Round your answer to the nearest tenth.

Problem 13
For this problem, consider 0 the smallest one-digit integer and 10 the smallest two-digit integer.

For how many two-digit integers is the product of their two digits a one-digit integer?

Problem 14

There are infinitely many pairs of integers A and B with $A, B \geq 2$ and
$$4 \cdot \log_B(A) = \log_A(B).$$
Consider the product $A \cdot B$ for these pairs. What is the smallest value of $A \cdot B > 100$?

Problem 15

Frank measures the wheel of his model car to have a circumference of 44 inches and a height of 14 inches. While painting the car, he accidentally spilled some paint on the top of the wheel as illustrated below:

Unfortunately, he doesn't notice until after he has moved his car forward 110 inches, getting some white paint on the floor. Frank is curious how far the spot of paint on the wheel is in its current position from where it was originally dropped on the wheel. Using Frank's measurements for the circumference and height of the wheel, assuming the car moved directly forward and the wheel did not slip, this distance can be written as $\sqrt{M}$ for an integer M. What is M?

Problem 16

A carnival game is played as follows. First you flip a fair coin. If heads you pick a ball from box A, which contains 3 green and 2 red balls. If tails you pick a ball from box B, which contains 1 green and 4 red balls. You win a prize if you pick a green ball.

Your friend plays first, getting heads and picking a winning ball. You play next, before the worker has a chance to replace the ball your friend picked. The probability you win can be written as $K\%$. What is K? Round your answer to the nearest hundredth.

Problem 17

Starting with a solid foam globe with radius 1 foot, Harry cuts off the top of the globe at the Arctic Circle to get the portion of the globe contained in the Arctic Circle. The Arctic Circle is at an angle of approximately 66.5° as shown below.

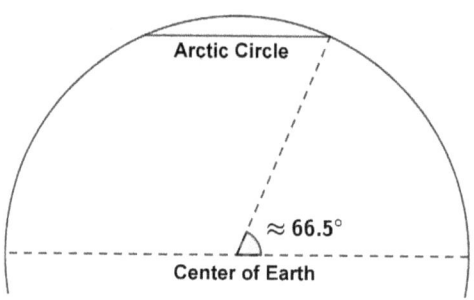

The base of the solid Harry cuts off is a circle. Using the approximations $\pi \approx \frac{22}{7}$ and $\tan(66.5°) \approx \frac{23}{10}$, the area of this base can be written as $\frac{P}{Q}$ for positive integers P and Q with $\gcd(P,Q) = 1$. What is $P + Q$?

Problem 18

For how many integer values of x is $y < 0$ for the graph

$$y = \sqrt{x+4} - \frac{8}{\sqrt{16-x}}?$$

1.7 ZIML April 2019 Division H

Problem 19
Let a function $f(n)$ be defined for all $n \geq 2$ as follows. For a prime p and positive integer k, then $f(p^k) = k+1$. Further, if $\gcd(n,m) = 1$, then $f(n \cdot m) = f(n) \cdot f(m)$. What is $f(9000)$?

Problem 20
Points A, B, C, and D are collinear (in that order) with $AB = 1$, $BC = 2$, and $CD = 3$ (hence $AD = 6$). Point E is such that $AE = \dfrac{\sqrt{58}}{2}$ and $DE = \dfrac{\sqrt{214}}{2}$. What is the perimeter of $\triangle BCE$? Round your answer to the nearest integer.

1.8 ZIML May 2019 Division H

Below are the 20 Problems from the Division H ZIML Competition held in May 2019.
The answer key is available on p.217 in the Appendix.
Full solutions to these questions are available starting on p.170.

Problem 1
In the diagram below, parallelograms $ABCD$ and $CEFH$ overlap to create rhombus $CDGH$.

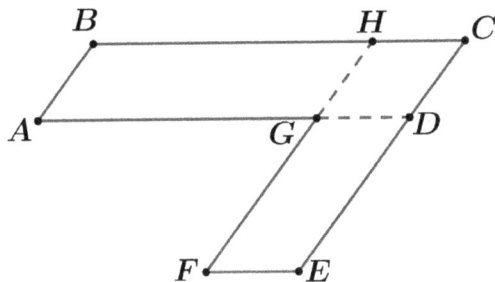

Suppose $AG : GD = 3 : 1$ and $FG : GH = 2 : 1$. If rhombus $CDGH$ has perimeter 8, what is the perimeter of the entire figure $ABCEFG$.

Problem 2

Greg is studying the effect of a certain gene on eye color in mice. The mice Greg is studying have either black or pink eyes. He makes the claim that "All mice with the gene have black eyes, and no mice without the gene have black eyes." He collects data from 150 mice as shown in the table below:

	Has Gene	Lacks Gene
Pink Eyes	30	70
Black Eyes	35	15

The probability that a randomly chosen mouse supports Greg's claim can be written as $P\%$. What is P, rounded to the nearest integer?

Problem 3

How many factors does the number $53 \cdot 54 \cdot 55$ have?

Problem 4

A cube has side lengths of 4 inches. A square pyramid is added to the top of the cube (whose base is the top of the cube), forming a new solid with 9 faces. Each of the lateral edges of the pyramid has length 3 inches.

Starting at one of the vertices of the cube, draw a path, following the edges of the solid, that contains all of the vertices of the solid. (The vertices at the start and end of the path are considered contained on the path.) What is the length, in inches, of the shortest such path?

Problem 5
What is the last digit of $7^{79} + 9^{79}$?

Problem 6
In a cube with side length 6, one vertex and two midpoints are used to create triangle $\triangle ABC$ as shown below:

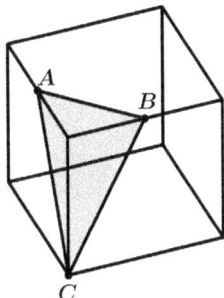

What is the area of this triangle? Round your answer to the nearest tenth.

Problem 7
K is a real number so that the equation $|x - 6| = 2\sqrt{x+K}$ has two real solutions. If $x = 2$ is one such solution, what is the other solution? Round your answer to the nearest tenth.

Problem 8

Line segment $\overline{AB}$ is tangent to a circle at B. The extension of the chord $\overline{CD}$ intersects $\overline{AB}$ at A, as shown in the diagram below, where $\angle BAC = 25°$ and (minor) arc $\widehat{BC}$ measures $55°$.

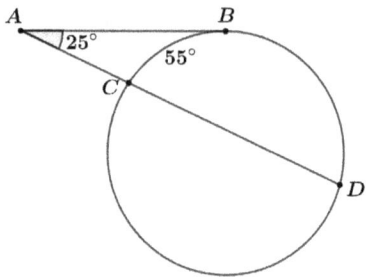

If the arc length of major arc $\widehat{CD}$ is 30π, then the area of the circle is $K \cdot \pi$ for an integer K. What is K?

Problem 9

Consider the graphs of $y = |5x|$ and $y = Mx - 1$ for integers M. For how many M do these graphs never intersect?

Problem 10
As part of a math project Kate came up with the equation

$$D(T) = 10{,}000 \cdot \left(\frac{64}{729}\right)^{T+2}$$

to model deforestation in her county. $D(T)$ represents the number of trees remaining, and T represents the number of quarters (3 month periods) from today.

There was nothing wrong with her model, but her teacher asked her to rewrite it in the form

$$D(t) = A \cdot \left(\frac{B}{C}\right)^t$$

for a real number A and positive integers B and C with $\gcd(B,C) = 1$. $D(t)$ still represents the number of trees remaining, but now t represents the number of months from today. If Kate rewrites her model in this form, what is $B+C$?

Problem 11
There is one value of M such that the circle $x^2 + y^2 = M$ is tangent to the line $y = 2x + 3$. What is M, rounded to the nearest tenth?

Problem 12
What is the largest 5-digit number of the form $\overline{A34BC}$ for digits A, B, and C that is divisible by 4, 5, and 9? Input the 5-digit number as your answer.

Problem 13
How many ways are there to write the numbers $1, 2, \ldots, 6$ in the 2×3 table below,

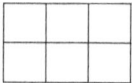

so that each row (left to right) and each column (top to bottom) is increasing?

For example,

1	4	5
3	2	6

is not allowed because the 2nd column decreases from 4 to 2 and the 2nd row decreases from 3 to 2.

Problem 14
The second largest angle in a hexagon is $126°$. If the 6 angles form an arithmetic sequence, what is the measure of the smallest angle?

Problem 15
Solve for x in the system of equations:

$$3x - 2\log_2(y) + 3^z = 5$$
$$2x + \log_2(y) - 3^z = 3$$
$$8x + \log_2(y) - 2 \cdot 3^z = 2$$

Round your answer to the nearest integer.

1.8 ZIML May 2019 Division H

Problem 16
There are finitely many integers m such that the graph of $y = x^2 - mx - 4m$ has no x-intercepts. What is the sum of all such m?

Problem 17
$x = 2 - i\sqrt{3}$ is a solution to the quadratic equation $x^2 + Bx + C = 0$ where B and C are integers. What is $B \cdot C$? Recall $i = \sqrt{-1}$.

Problem 18
Logan picks 4 cards without replacement from a set of 30 cards. The order Logan picks the cards does not matter. These cards consist of three different colors, each numbered $1, 2, \ldots, 10$. The probability that Logan's cards are all the same color and consist of 4 consecutive numbers (such as $2, 3, 4, 5$) can be written as $\dfrac{P}{Q}$ for positive integers P and Q with $\gcd(P, Q) = 1$. What is $Q - P$?

Problem 19
There are infinitely many pairs of integers M and N such that
$$\log_{1/5}(\log_2 M) = \log_{1/2}(\log_5 N).$$
One such pair has $M = 2 \cdot 8^8$. For this M, what is N?

Problem 20

Right triangle $\triangle ADE$ is drawn inside right triangle $\triangle ABC$ as shown in the diagram below (which is not drawn to scale).

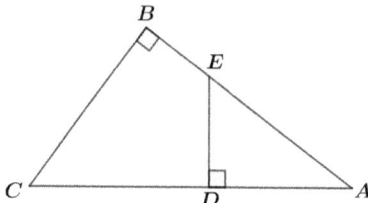

Given $BC = 8$, $AE = CD$, and $\cos(\angle A) = \dfrac{\sqrt{5}}{3}$, the length AE can be expressed as $S + T\sqrt{5}$ for integers S and T. What is $S + T$?

1.9 ZIML June 2019 Division H

Below are the 20 Problems from the Division H ZIML Competition held in June 2019.
The answer key is available on p.218 in the Appendix.
Full solutions to these questions are available starting on p.184.

Problem 1
A right triangle, a regular pentagon, and a regular hexagon are drawn sharing vertex A as in the diagram below.

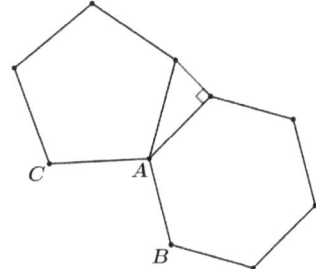

If the pentagon has a side length of 4 and the hexagon has a side length of $2\sqrt{3}$, what is angle $\angle BAC$, measured in degrees with $\angle BAC < 180°$? Round your answer to the nearest degree.

Problem 2
How many ways are there to arrange the letters of SUMMERTIME so that the vowels are in alphabetical order? (Remember A, E, I, O, and U are the vowels.)

Problem 3

$x = -2$, $x = \dfrac{2}{3}$, and $x = \pm 2i$ are all zeros of the polynomial

$$P(x) = 12x^4 + Bx^3 + Cx^2 + Dx + E.$$

What is $B + C + D + E$?

Problem 4

Liliana just started teaching a cooking class for 20 people, 11 of them female. Students were supposed to bring an apron and a chef's hat to class. The first day of class everyone forgot something, but no one forbot both their apron and their hat. Liliana counted that 5 males and 3 females forgot to bring their apron.

If we randomly choose one student who forgot their hat, the probability that the student is male is $\dfrac{P}{Q}$ as a fraction in lowest terms. What is $Q - P$?

Problem 5
Three 30-60-90 triangles (labeled A, C, and E) and two 45-45-90 triangles (labeled B and D) are drawn as in the diagram below.

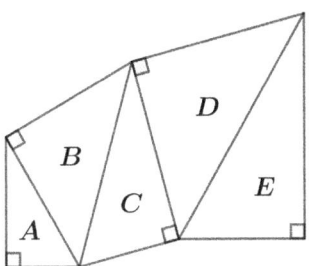

If the area of triangle A is 90, what is the area of triangle E? Round your answer to the nearest integer.

Problem 6
There is a unique rational solution to the equation

$$64^{3x+2} = 128^{x-4}$$

with the form $\dfrac{P}{Q}$ for integers P and Q with $Q > 0$ and $\gcd(P, Q) = 1$. What is $Q - P$?

Problem 7
For how many integers M is the maximum value of $y = -x^2 + Mx - 3$ less than M?

Problem 8
Let $ABCD$ be a rectangle with $AB = 10$. Let E be the midpoint of side BC and F be the midpoint of side CD.

If $\angle AEF = 90°$, $AD = \sqrt{K}$ for some integer K. What is K?

Problem 9
What is the remainder when 6^{5050} is divided by 50?

Problem 10
Diameters $\overline{AB}$ and $\overline{CD}$ intersect as in the diagram below.

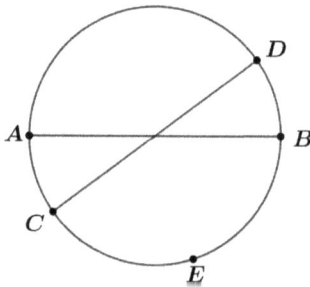

Minor arcs $\widehat{DB}$, $\widehat{BE}$, and $\widehat{EC}$ satisfy

$$2 \cdot m\widehat{DB} = m\widehat{BE} = m\widehat{EC}.$$

What is the largest angle in $\triangle ADE$? Give your answer in degrees, rounded to the nearest degree.

1.9 ZIML June 2019 Division H

Problem 11
Consider the roots that are possible roots to the equation

$$(x-1)(2x+1)(x-3)(x+3) = 0$$

according to the Rational Root Theorem. $K\%$ of these possible roots are actual roots. What is K rounded to the nearest integer?

Problem 12
A cone has a height h and a radius r. If it has the same volume as a sphere with radius $\frac{r}{3}$, then the ratio $\frac{h}{r}$ can be written as $\frac{P}{Q}$ for positive integers P and Q with $\gcd(P,Q) = 1$. What is $P+Q$?

Problem 13
A, B, and C are events with $P(A) = 0.4$, $P(B) = 0.3$, and $P(C) = 0.2$. A and B are mutually exclusive (or disjoint), but $P(A \cap C) = P(B \cap C) = 0.1$. What is $P(A \cup B \cup C)$?

Problem 14

Find the largest 5-digit integer $\overline{abcde}$ so that:

(i) 2 is a factor of the 1-digit number $\overline{a}$,

(ii) 2 and 3 are factors of the 2-digit number $\overline{ab}$,

(iii) 2, 3, and 4 are factors of the 3-digit number $\overline{abc}$,

(iv) 2, 3, 4, and 5 are factors of the 4-digit number $\overline{abcd}$,

(v) 2, 3, 4, 5, and 6 are factors of the 5-digit number $\overline{abcde}$.

Problem 15

Let ABC be an acute triangle with $AB = 12$, $AC = 17$ and $\sin(A) = \dfrac{2\sqrt{42}}{17}$. What is BC? Round your answer to the nearest integer if necessary.

Problem 16

What is the y-value of the vertex of the parabola containing the points $(2,5)$, $(6,5)$, and $(7,6)$? Round your answer to the nearest tenth.

Problem 17
Four squares, with side length 1, 2, 3, and 4 are drawn as in the diagram below, with line segment $\overline{BC}$ connecting the lower left corner to the upper right corner.

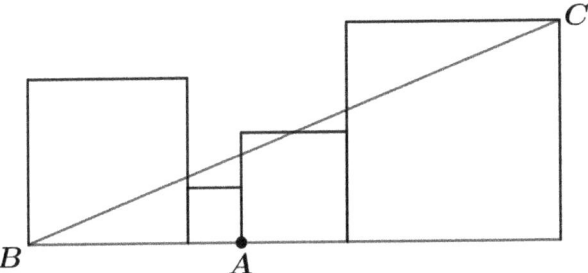

The distance from point A to $\overline{BC}$ can be written as $\dfrac{R\sqrt{S}}{T}$ for positive integers R, S, and T with S square-free and $\gcd(R,T)=1$. What is $R+S+T$?

Problem 18
One problem on Ralph's math test asked him to multiply a complex number $a+bi$ by $4-i$. Ralph accidentally added $4-i$ to $a+bi$. To his surprise, Ralph got the question correct. What is a^2+b^2, rounded to the nearest tenth?

Problem 19

Consider the graph of the piecewise function

$$f(x) = \begin{cases} 0.5x + 2, & \text{if } x < 3 \\ 5 - x, & \text{if } x \geq 3 \end{cases}$$

What is the area below this graph and above the x-axis? Round your answer to the nearest hundredth.

Problem 20

Define the function $f(x)$ as follows. Given x, first find the prime factorization of x. Then, for each prime in this factorization, swap the base and the exponent. For example,

$$f(200) = f(2^3 \cdot 5^2) = 3^2 \cdot 2^5 = 288.$$

How many factors does $f(144)$ have?

2. ZIML Solutions

This part of the book contains the official solutions to the problems from the nine Division H ZIML Contests from the 2018-19 School Year.

Students are encouraged to discuss and share their own methods to the problems using the Discussion Forum on ziml.areteem.org.

2.1 ZIML October 2018 Division H

Below are the solutions from the Division H ZIML Competition held in October 2018.
The problems from the contest are available on p.17.

Problem 1 Solution

If we let $A = 2$, $B = -4$, and $C = 1$, note Barry solves the equation $Ax^2 + Bx + C = 0$ and Cary solves the equation $Cx^2 + Bx + A$. Thus, using the quadratic formula, the roots of Barry's equation and Cary's equation are

$$\frac{-B \pm \sqrt{B^2 - 4AC}}{2A} \text{ and } \frac{-B \pm \sqrt{B^2 - 4CA}}{2C},$$

using the quadratic formula. Note these are the same except for their denominators. Therefore the ratio of the larger roots (the + in the $\pm$ of the quadratic formula) is

$$\left(\frac{-B \pm \sqrt{B^2 - 4AC}}{2A}\right) \div \left(\frac{-B \pm \sqrt{B^2 - 4CA}}{2C}\right) = \frac{2C}{2A} = \frac{C}{A}.$$

We have $\frac{C}{A} = \frac{1}{2}$ and hence our final answer is 0.5.

Answer: 0.5

Problem 2 Solution

If Mr. Lang first has spots for the girls, this creates 11 gaps for the boys, as seen below:

$$\_G\_G\_G\_ \cdots \_G\_.$$

Mr. Lang must then choose 5 of these spots for the boys. As the order doesn't matter, this can be done in $\binom{11}{5} = \frac{11!}{5! \cdot 6!} = 462$ ways.

Answer: 462

2.1 ZIML October 2018 Division H

Problem 3 Solution

Let x be the eastern field's length in yards, so its width is $x - 700$ yards. The second field's length is $x - 450$ yards. Since they are of the same area, we have equation $x(x - 700) = (x - 450) \times 400$. This equation simplifies to

$$x^2 - 1100x + 180000 = 0$$

It can be factored into $(x - 200)(x - 900) = 0$, and has solutions $x = 200$ and $x = 900$. The solution $x = 200$ does not make sense (else the western field has a length of -250 yards!).

Hence the eastern field is 900 yards by 200 yards while the western field is 450 yards by 400 yards. The total amount of fence Jane needs is

$$2 \times (900 + 200) + 2 \times (450 + 400) = 3900$$

yards, the sum of the perimeters.

Answer: 3900

Problem 4 Solution

$y = 4\sqrt{x} - 1$ is undefined for $x < 0$ so if the two graphs intersect at a point where $y \geq 0$, we must have $m \geq 0$. We have

$$mx = 4\sqrt{x} - 1 \Rightarrow mx + 1 = 4\sqrt{x} \Rightarrow m^2x^2 + 2mx + 1 = 16x$$

after squaring both sides. Therefore $m^2x^2 + (2m - 16)x + 1 = 0$. Using the discriminant, this has solutions when

$$(2m - 16)^2 - 4 \cdot m^2 \geq 0 \Rightarrow 4m^2 - 64m + 256 - 4m^2 \geq 0.$$

Solving we have $64m \leq 256$ or $m \leq 4$. As we also have $m \geq 0$, $m = 0, 1, 2, 3, 4$, and hence 5 integer m values are possible.

Answer: 5

Problem 5 Solution

Since the sequence is geometric, it has formula $a_n = 12 \cdot 18^n$.

Looking at the prime factorization we have $a_n = 2^2 \cdot 3 \cdot (2 \cdot 3^2)^n = 2^{2+n} \cdot 3^{1+2n}$. For this to be a perfect cube, both the exponents $2+n$ and $1+2n$ must be a multiple of 3.

Finding a pattern we see that $n = 1, 4, 7, \ldots$ (every third term) will work. Hence $a_1, a_4, \ldots, a_{97}$ are all perfect cubes, a total of $(97-1) \div 3 + 1 = 33$ terms.

Answer: 33

Problem 6 Solution

The angles in $\triangle ABC$ add up to 180°, so $\angle A + \angle B = 180° - 15° = 165°$. Let k such that $\dfrac{\angle A}{\angle B} = \dfrac{8k}{3k}$ so $8k + 3k = 165°$ and hence $k = 165 \div 11 = 15°$. Thus $\angle A = 8 \cdot 15° = 120°$ and $\angle B = 3 \cdot 15° = 45°$.

Using the Law of Sines we have

$$\frac{\sin(A)}{a} = \frac{\sin(B)}{b} \Rightarrow \frac{a}{b} = \frac{\sin(A)}{\sin(B)} = \frac{\sin(120°)}{\sin(45°)} = \frac{\sqrt{3}/2}{\sqrt{2}/2} = \frac{\sqrt{3}}{\sqrt{2}}.$$

Thus the ratio $\dfrac{a^2}{b^2} = \left(\dfrac{\sqrt{3}}{\sqrt{2}}\right)^2 = \dfrac{3}{2}$ so $N + M = 3 + 2 = 5$.

Answer: 5

Problem 7 Solution

Using the change of base formula, $\log_{1/2}(x) = \dfrac{\log_2(x)}{\log_2(1/2)} = -\log_2(x)$. Therefore, where our equation is defined it is equivalent to $\log_4(x^2) = 4$. Solving for x we have $x^2 = 4^4$ so $x = \pm\sqrt{256} = \pm 16$.

2.1 ZIML October 2018 Division H

Note, however, that our equation is not defined for $x < 0$. Therefore $x = 16$ is the only solution, hence the smallest.

Answer: 16

Problem 8 Solution

In total Peter has $3 \cdot 3 \cdot 2 = 18$ choices for what to wear to the ceremony.

As Peter can choose the same piece of clothing, but not the exact same set of clothes for the reception, he thus has $18 - 1 = 17$ choices for what to wear to the reception.

Peter must decide what to wear for both, so he has $18 \cdot 17 = 306$ choices in total.

Answer: 306

Problem 9 Solution

We have $\sin(2x) = 2\sin(x) \cdot \cos(x)$. Hence

$$\begin{aligned} 4\sin^2(x) + 2\sin(2x) &= 4\sin^2(x) + 4\sin(x)\cos(x) \\ &= 4\sin(x)(\sin(x) + \cos(x)) \\ &= 0. \end{aligned}$$

Thus either $\sin(x) = 0$ or $\sin(x) + \cos(x) = 0$.

In the first case, $x = 180° \cdot k$ for integers k. For $0° \leq x \leq 1000°$ we have $0 \leq k \leq 5$, a total of 6 possibilities.

In the second case, $\sin(x) = -\cos(x)$ or $\tan(x) = -1$, hence $x = 135° + 180° \cdot k$ for integers k. For $0° \leq x \leq 1000°$ we have $0 \leq k \leq 4$, a total of 5 possibilities.

Therefore in total we have $6 + 5 = 11$ solutions for $0° \leq x \leq$

$1000°$.

Answer: 11

Problem 10 Solution
The surface area of the prism is made up of triangles $\triangle ABC$, $\triangle ABF$, $\triangle CBF$ and $\triangle ACF$.

$\triangle ABC \cong \triangle ABF \cong \triangle CBF$ and each have an area of $\frac{1}{2} \cdot 2 \cdot 2 = 2$.

$\triangle ACF$ is an equilateral triangle with sides of length $2\sqrt{2} = \sqrt{8}$, so using the given approximation has area $\frac{1.7 \cdot (\sqrt{8})^2}{4} = 1.7 \cdot 2 = 3.4$.

Hence the surface area of the prism is $2 \cdot 3 + 3.4 = 9.4$.

Answer: 9.4

Problem 11 Solution
We know $45 = 5 \cdot 9$, so the number must be divisible by 5 and by 9. To be divisible by 5, either $B = 0$ or $B = 5$. To be divisible by 9, the sum of the digits, $1 + 2 + A + 4 + B = A + B + 7$ must be divisible by 9.

First suppose $B = 0$. To be divisible by 9, the sum of the digits must be divisible by 9. The sum of the digits is $A + 0 + 7 = A + 7$. As A is a digit, $A + 7 = 9$ so $A = 2$. However, this five-digit number 12240 has repeated digits.

Next suppose $B = 5$. The sum of the digits here is $A + 5 + 7 = A + 12$. As A is a digit, $A + 12 = 18$ so $A = 6$. This gives the five-digit number 12645 with no repeated digits. Hence 12645 is the answer.

Answer: 12645

2.1 ZIML October 2018 Division H

Problem 12 Solution
Using polynomial long division we have that

$$(x^4+2x^2+3x+4) \div (x^2-3) = (x^2+5) \text{ with remainder } (3x+19).$$

To find the zero, $3x+19 = 0$ or $x = \dfrac{-19}{3}$. Thus $Q - P = 3 - (-19) = 22$.

Answer: 22

Problem 13 Solution
The perpendicular bisector of $\overline{OA}$ has slope $-\dfrac{1}{2}$. As it contains $(7.5, 0)$ it has equation

$$y - 0 = -\frac{1}{2}(x - 7.5) = -x + 3.75.$$

Solving $y = 2x$ and $y = -0.5x + 3.75$ we get $2.5x = 3.75$ or $x = 1.5$, giving the midpoint of $\overline{OA}$ as $(1.5, 3)$. Since $O = (0,0)$ we must have $A = (1.5 \cdot 2, 3 \cdot 2) = (3, 6)$. Hence the y-value of A is 6.

Answer: 6

Problem 14 Solution
The prime factorizations of the relevant numbers are $504 = 2^3 \cdot 3^2 \cdot 7$, $14 = 2 \cdot 7$, $84 = 2^2 \cdot 3 \cdot 7$, and $420 = 2^2 \cdot 3 \cdot 5 \cdot 7$.

Looking at $\text{lcm}(N, 84) = 420$ we know that the prime factorization of N must be $2^x \cdot 3^y \cdot 5^1 \cdot 7^z$ where x equals 0, 1, or 2, y equals 0 or 1, and z equals 0 or 1. (As the least common multiple is divisible by 5 but 28 is not, N must be divisible by 5.)

We now examine $\gcd(N, 504) = 14$. N and 42 share 14 as a common factor (but not 3). Further, N is not divisible by 4. Hence the prime factorization of N has exactly one 2, zero 3's, and at least one 7. Combined with the above restrictions, we have $N = 2^1 \cdot 3^0 \cdot 5^1 \cdot 7^1 = 70$ as our answer.

Answer: 70

Problem 15 Solution
Using (x, y, z) coordinates, let $(0,0,0)$ be Fred's position, with the positive y-axis denoting north.

As the drone starts by traveling straight north at an angle of elevation of $30°$, after the 200 meter flight it ends at position $(0, 200\cos(30°), 200\sin(30°)) = (0, 100\sqrt{3}, 100)$. (Note you can also do this calculation using a 30-60-90 right triangle.)

Thus, after a 400 meter flight due west, the drone is at position $(-400, 100\sqrt{3}, 100)$. Using the distance formula this is

$$\sqrt{(-400)^2 + (100\sqrt{3})^2 + (100)^2}$$
$$= \sqrt{160,000 + 30,000 + 10,000}$$
$$= \sqrt{200,000}$$

meters from Fred. Therefore $K = 200,000$.

Answer: 200000

Problem 16 Solution
The area of the field is a $60°$ sector and two (congruent) triangles. The area of the sector is

$$\frac{60°}{360°} \pi \cdot 400^2 \approx \frac{3}{6} \cdot 400^2 = 80,000 \text{ sq. ft.}$$

The two triangles each have sides of 325 ft and 400 ft, with an angle of $(90° - 60°) \div 2$ between them. Hence their combined area is

$$2 \cdot \left(\frac{1}{2} \cdot 400 \cdot 325 \cdot \sin(15°)\right) \approx 400 \cdot 325 \cdot 0.25 = 32,500.$$

2.1 ZIML October 2018 Division H

Hence the field's area is approximately

$$80,000 + 32,500 = 112,500$$

square feet.

Answer: 112500

Problem 17 Solution
Since $\sqrt{5}$ is a solution, so is $-\sqrt{5}$. Similarly, we have $1 \pm i$ are solutions. Therefore the polynomial

$$x^4 + Bx^3 + Cx^2 + Dx - 10$$
$$= (x - \sqrt{5})(x + \sqrt{5})(x - (1+i))(x - (1-i))$$
$$= (x^2 - 5)(x^2 - 2x + 2)$$
$$= x^4 - 2x^3 - 3x^2 + 10x - 10$$

so $B = -3$.

Answer: -3

Problem 18 Solution
Call the intersection of $\overline{AC}$ and $\overline{BE}$ point F. Using $\triangle BCF$, $\angle CBE = 180° - x° - 3x° = 180° - 4x°$. Therefore,

$$\widehat{CE} = 2\angle CBE = 360° - 8x°.$$

As $\overline{AD} \parallel \overline{BC}$, $\angle CAD = \angle ACB = x°$ so $\widehat{CD} = 2x°$. Thus

$$\widehat{CE} = \widehat{CD} + \widehat{DE} = 2x° + 30°.$$

Hence we have $2x° + 30° = 360° - 8x°$ so solving for x we get $x = 33$.

Answer: 33

Problem 19 Solution

There are $6 \cdot 10 = 60$ outcomes in total.

For the number of outcomes where Terry's roll is larger than Sierra's, consider cases based on Sierra's roll. If Sierra rolls a 1, Terry can roll 2 through 10, a total of 9 outcomes. Similarly if Sierra rolls a $2, 3, \ldots 6$, there $7, 6, \ldots 4$ outcomes. In total this gives $9 + 8 + 7 + 6 + 5 + 4 = 39$ outcomes where Terry's roll is larger than Sierras.

This gives a final probability of $\dfrac{39}{60} = \dfrac{13}{20}$ so $B - A = 7$.

Answer: 7

Problem 20 Solution

We know $pq = -4$ and $p - q = 2$. Substituting $q = p - 2$ we have $p(p-2) = -4$ or $p^2 - 2p + 4 = 0$. Using the quadratic formula we have

$$p = \frac{2 \pm \sqrt{4 - 4 \cdot 4}}{2} = \frac{2 \pm \sqrt{-12}}{2} = 1 \pm i\sqrt{3}.$$

As p is of the form $A + i\sqrt{B}$ for positive integers A and B, we have $p = 1 + i\sqrt{3}$ so $A + B = 1 + 3 = 4$.

Answer: 4

2.2 ZIML November 2018 Division H

Below are the solutions from the Division H ZIML Competition held in November 2018.
The problems from the contest are available on p.25.

Problem 1 Solution
Multiplying by $4x$ to clear denominators we have

$$16x + 4x^2 + 4 = 16x^2 + 1.$$

Collecting like terms we have

$$12x^2 - 16x - 3 = (2x-3)(6x+1) = 0$$

and hence $x = \frac{3}{2}$ or $x = -\frac{1}{6}$. As P and Q must be positive, we have $P + Q = 3 + 2 = 5$.

Answer: 5

Problem 2 Solution
If one internal angle is $x°$, we know one external angle is $180° - x°$. As the smallest internal angle for a regular polygon is $60°$ (for an equilateral triangle) we know the internal angle must be larger than the external angle.

Each internal angle of a regular polygon with n sides is $\frac{180(n-2)}{n}$. Thus,

$$\frac{180(n-2)}{n} - \left(180° - \frac{180(n-2)}{n}\right) = 164.$$

Distributing, clearing denominators, and simplifying we have $16n = 720$ so $n = 45$.

Answer: 45

Problem 3 Solution

If she flips the coin twice there is a $1 - \frac{1}{4} = \frac{3}{4}$ chance that she'll get at least one heads, and if she flips the coin three times there is a $1 - \frac{1}{8} = \frac{7}{8}$ chance that she'll get at least one heads.

Thus, using the Law of Total Probability, the probability that she gets at least one heads is

$$\frac{3}{4} \times \frac{2}{3} + \frac{7}{8} \times \frac{1}{3} = \frac{19}{24}.$$

Therefore, $P + Q = 19 + 24 = 43$.

Answer: 43

Problem 4 Solution

Ignoring the square root, we know $x^2 - 18x + 98$ is a quadratic. It's minimum will occur at the vertex, when

$$x = -\frac{b}{2a} = -\frac{-18}{2} = 9.$$

Hence the minimum value of $x^2 - 18x + 98$ will be

$$9^2 - 18 \cdot 9 + 98 = 9(9 - 18) + 98 = -81 + 98 = 17.$$

Therefore, the smallest value of $f(x)$ will be $f(9) = \sqrt{17}$. As $4 < \sqrt{17} < 5$ the smallest integer output by Patrick's program will be 4.

Answer: 4

Problem 5 Solution

We know that any median divides a triangle into two triangles of equal area, each with half the area of the original triangle.

2.2 ZIML November 2018 Division H

Using that EF is a median of $\triangle BED$, ED is a median of $\triangle BEC$, and BE is a median of $\triangle ABC$ we thus have (here $[DEF]$ is used to denote the area of $\triangle DEF$, etc.):

$$[DEF] = \frac{1}{2}[BED]$$
$$= \frac{1}{2}\left(\frac{1}{2}[BEC]\right) = \frac{1}{4}[BEC]$$
$$= \frac{1}{4}\left(\frac{1}{2}[ABC]\right) = \frac{1}{8}[ABC]$$

so $[DEF] : [ABC] = 1 : 8$ and $P + Q = 1 + 8 = 9$.

Answer: 9

Problem 6 Solution
We first find the prime factorization: $43560 = 2^3 \cdot 3^2 \cdot 5 \cdot 11^2$. Note divisibility rules for 9 and 11 help a lot here.

Therefore 43560 has $(3+1)(2+1)(1+1)(2+1) = 72$ factors.

Answer: 72

Problem 7 Solution
The volume of a sphere with radius r is $\frac{4}{3}\pi r^3$. As

$$166.67\pi \approx 166\frac{2}{3}\pi = \frac{500}{3}\pi$$

we solve the equation

$$\frac{500}{3}\pi = \frac{4}{3}\pi r^3$$

to get $r^3 = 125$ or $r = 5$. Therefore Dylan removed a sphere of radius 5 from the center of the pumpkin.

Thus the full pumpkin has a radius of $5+2=7$ inches and a volume of
$$\frac{4}{3}\pi \cdot 7^3 = \frac{4}{3}\pi \cdot 343 = \frac{1372}{3}\pi.$$
Hence the remaining volume is
$$\frac{1372}{3}\pi - \frac{500}{3}\pi = \frac{872}{3}\pi$$
and $P = \frac{872}{3} \approx 290.67$.

Answer: 290.67

Problem 8 Solution
Let (minor) arc $\widehat{AC}$ have measure $x°$ and (minor) arc $\widehat{BD}$ have measure y.

Using $\angle AEC = 26°$ we have $\frac{x-y}{2} = 26$ so $x - y = 52$. Noting that AD and BC intersect at a $62°$ angle we also have $\frac{x+y}{2} = 62$ so $x + y = 124$.

To solve for x, add the two equations, giving $2x = 124 + 52 = 176$. Therefore $x = \widehat{AC} = 88°$.

Answer: 88

Problem 9 Solution
Using the change of base formula we have (here $\log(x)$ denotes $\log_{10}(x)$ but the below argument works for any base)
$$\log_5(6) = \frac{\log(6)}{\log(5)}, \log_6(7) = \frac{\log(7)}{\log(6)}, \ldots$$

2.2 ZIML November 2018 Division H

Therefore we have

$$\log_5(6) \cdot \log_6(7) \cdot \log_7(8) \cdots \log_{n-1}(n)$$
$$= \frac{\log(6)}{\log(5)} \cdot \frac{\log(7)}{\log(6)} \cdots \frac{\log(n)}{\log(n-1)}$$
$$= \frac{\log(n)}{\log(5)}$$
$$= \log_5(n)$$

Thus, our product is an integer if and only if n is a power of 5. There are 3 powers of 5 ($25, 125, 625$) in our range, hence there are 3 values of n so that the product is an integer.

Answer: 3

Problem 10 Solution
Note he each time he adds squares to his rectangle, he adds 2 more squares than the previous time.

Thus, when he draws his 11th rectangle he has $2 + 6 + 10 + \cdots + 22 = 72$ white squares and $4 + 8 + 12 + 16 + 20 = 60$ black squares.

Answer: 72

Problem 11 Solution
We consider two cases, either $2x^2 - 29 = 21$ or $2x^2 - 29 = -21$.

In the first case we have $2x^2 = 50$ so $x^2 = 25$ and hence $x = \pm 5$. Checking, both of these solutions work.

In the second case we similarly have $2x^2 - 29 = -21$ so $2x^2 = 8$ and $x^2 = 4$. This gives two more solutions of $x = \pm 2$.

Therefore the product of all integer solutions is $(-25) \cdot (-4) =$

100.

Answer: 100

Problem 12 Solution
Clearly the area of $ABCD$ is the sum of the areas of $\triangle ABD$ and $\triangle BCD$. As we know two sides and the angle of each, we can calculate their areas using sine. The area of $\triangle ABD$ is

$$\frac{1}{2} \cdot 6 \cdot 4 \cdot \sin 60° = 12 \cdot \frac{\sqrt{3}}{2} = 6\sqrt{3}.$$

Similarly the area of $\triangle BCD$ is

$$\frac{1}{2} \cdot 2 \cdot 4 \cdot \sin 60° = 4 \cdot \frac{\sqrt{3}}{2} = 2\sqrt{3}.$$

Hence the area of $ABCD$ is $(2+6)\sqrt{3} = 8\sqrt{3}$. Writing under a single square root we have $\sqrt{64 \cdot 3} = \sqrt{192}$ and thus $M = 192$.

Answer: 192

Problem 13 Solution
Note $18 = 2 \cdot 3^2$, so the smallest perfect square that is a multiple of 18 is $2^2 \cdot 3^2 = 36$. Hence any perfect square that is a multiple of 18 can be written as $36 \cdot K^2 = (6 \cdot K)^2$ for an integer K.

We know Jared listed all the perfect squares $1^2, 2^2, \ldots, 100^2$ so we can count the multiples of 6 less than 100. As $100 \div 6 = 16$ with remainder 4, there are 16 multiples of 6 less than 100. Therefore there are 16 multiples of 18 in the perfect squares Jared lists.

(For reference, they are $6^2 = 36, 12^2 = 144, \ldots, 96^2 = 9216$.)

Answer: 16

2.2 ZIML November 2018 Division H

Problem 14 Solution

If $f^{-1}(1357) = K$, then $f(K) = 1357$. Hence

$$K^3 + 2K + 4 = 1357 \text{ or } K(K^2 + 2) = 1353.$$

Since K is an integer, K is a factor of $1353 = 3 \cdot 11 \cdot 41$. Testing these factors, we see $K = 11$ works (with $K^2 + 2 = 123 = 3 \cdot 41$).

Answer: 11

Problem 15 Solution

For the circle to be tangent to both axes, the center must be the same distance from both axes. Since the center is on the line $y = 12 - 3x$, it will have coordinates $(x, 12 - 3x)$ for some x. Hence we need

$$x = 12 - 3x \Rightarrow 4x = 12 \Rightarrow x = 3.$$

Therefore the center has coordinates $(3, 3)$ with radius 3 as well. This gives the equation

$$(x - 3)^2 + (y - 3)^2 = 3^2$$
$$x^2 - 6x + 9 + y^2 - 6y + 9 = 9$$
$$x^2 + y^2 - 6x - 6y + 9 = 0$$

Hence $A + B + C + D + E = 1 + 1 - 6 - 6 + 9 = -1$.

Answer: -1

Problem 16 Solution

We first calculate points B, C, and D. They are

$$B = A \cdot 2i = (1 + i) \cdot 2i = -2 + 2i,$$
$$C = B \cdot 2i = (-2 + 2i) \cdot 2i = -4 - 4i,$$
$$D = C \cdot 2i = (-4 - 4i) \cdot 2i = 8 - 8i.$$

As points in the complex plane we have

$$A = (1,1), B = (-2,2), C = (-4,-4), \text{ and } D = (8,-8).$$

Note A and C are on the line $y = x$ and B and D are on the line $y = -x$. Hence in fact the diagonals of $ABCD$ are perpendicular so $ABCD$ is a kite.

The area of $ABCD$ is therefore $AC \cdot BD \div 2$. We have

$$AC = \sqrt{(1-(-4))^2 + (1-(-4))^2} = \sqrt{50} = 5\sqrt{2}$$
$$BD = \sqrt{(-2-8)^2 + (2-(-8))^2} = \sqrt{200} = 10\sqrt{2}$$

so the area of $ABCD$ is $5\sqrt{2} \cdot 10\sqrt{2} \div 2 = 50$.

Answer: 50

Problem 17 Solution

Since the hexagon is regular, cutting off the two triangles produces a rectangle as shown in the diagram below.

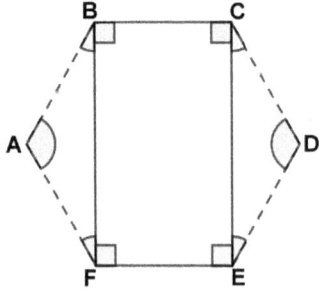

Both $\triangle ABF$ and $\triangle CDE$ are isosceles triangles with angles $30°$, $30°$, $120°$. Hence they can each be split into 30-60-90 triangles with sides $3, 3\sqrt{2}, 6$. Therefore we have

$$BC = EF = 6 \text{ and } BF = CE = 2 \cdot 3\sqrt{2} = 6\sqrt{3}.$$

Hence the area of $BCEF$ is $6 \cdot 6\sqrt{3} = 36\sqrt{3}$ and $R + S = 36 + 3 = 39$.

Answer: 39

Problem 18 Solution

Monica has $\binom{8}{2} = 28$ ways to choose the two candy bars and $\binom{11}{3} = 165$ ways to choose the 3 remaining candy.

Thus, Monica has $28 \times 165 = 4620$ ways to choose which collection of candy to bring to the game.

Answer: 4620

Problem 19 Solution

First we note this is equivalent to finding the units digit of

$$8^{31} + 1^{31} + 2^{31} + 2^{31} + 5^{31} + 3^{31} + 5^{31} + 5^{31} + 4^{31}.$$

Hence we need to find the patterns in the units digit for powers of 1, 2, 3, 4, 5, and 8. We summarize these patterns in the table below

Digit	Pattern of Powers
1	1, ...
2	2, 4, 8, 6, ...
3	3, 9, 7, 1, ...
4	4, 6, ...
5	5, ...
8	8, 4, 2, 6, ...

Clearly 1^{31} has units digit 1 and 5^{31} has units digit 5. As 31 is odd, 4^{31} has units digit 4. The other patterns repeat every 4 terms, so as $31 \div 4$ has remainder 3, each is the 3rd value in the pattern: 2^{31} has units digit 8, 3^{31} has units digit 7, and 8^{31} has units digit 2.

Putting this all together we have the units digit of our expression is the units digit of

$$2+1+8+8+5+7+5+5+4 = 45$$

so our answer is 5.

Answer: 5

Problem 20 Solution

First we substitute the double angle for tangent

$$\tan(\theta) \cdot \frac{2\tan(\theta)}{1-\tan^2(\theta)} = -3.$$

Clearing denominators and combining like terms we have

$$-\tan^2(\theta) = -3 \Rightarrow \tan(\theta) = \pm\frac{\sqrt{3}}{3}.$$

We thus have (recall we are restricting to $0° \leq \theta < 360°$)

$$\tan(\theta) = \frac{\sqrt{3}}{3} \Rightarrow \theta = 60°, 240°$$

$$\tan(\theta) = -\frac{\sqrt{3}}{3} \Rightarrow \theta = 120°, 300°$$

Hence the difference between the largest and smallest solution is $300° - 60° = 240°$ so our answer is 240.

Answer: 240

2.3 ZIML December 2018 Division H

Below are the solutions from the Division H ZIML Competition held in December 2018.
The problems from the contest are available on p.33.

Problem 1 Solution
Consider the diagram below, where radii are drawn for each of the 4 circles to the intersection points.

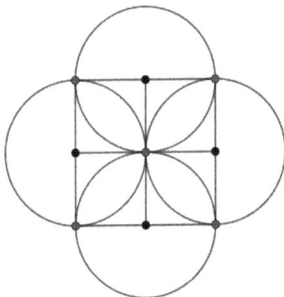

Since the opposite circles are tangent, this divides the full region into 4 squares (each with side length 1) and 4 semicircles (each with radius 1). Therefore the area is

$$4 \times (1^2) + 4 \times \left(\frac{1}{2}\pi 1^2\right) = 4 + 2\pi.$$

Using $\pi \approx 3.14$ this is $4 + 2 \times 3.14 = 10.28$.

Answer: 10.28

Problem 2 Solution
Expanding we have

$$x^6 - 8x^3 - 128 = 0,$$

so the equation is quadratic in x^3. Let $z = x^3$, we have $z^2 - 8z - 128 = 0$. Factoring, $(z+8)(z-16) = 0$, so $z = -8$ or $z = 16$. $x^3 = -8$ gives integer solution -2 while $x^3 = 16$ has no integer solutions. Hence our answer is -2.

Answer: -2

Problem 3 Solution

Thus far Julie has the 5 numbers $0, 1, 3, 5, 7$. We know that last two numbers are at most 8 and at least 0.

If both numbers are 8, then the 7 numbers are

$$0, 1, 3, 5, 7, 8, 8$$

and the largest median $L = 5$.

If both numbers are 0, then the 7 numbers are

$$0, 0, 0, 1, 3, 5, 7$$

and the smallest median $S = 1$.

Therefore $L - S = 5 - 1 = 4$.

Answer: 4

Problem 4 Solution

We estimate each logarithm first. Note $2^7 = 128$, so $\log_2(123)$ is slightly less than 7.

$3^5 = 243$ so $\log_3(246)$ is slightly more than 5.

Similar reasoning gives $\log_4(1023) \approx 5$ and $\log_5(3210) \approx 5$.

This gives a final estimate of $7 + 5 + 5 + 5 = 22$.

(In fact, the expression is approximately 21.97, so our estimate is accurate to the nearest tenth.)

Answer: 22

Problem 5 Solution
Using the intersecting lines it is easy to calculate

$$A = (0,0), B = (6,3), \text{ and } C = \left(-\frac{3}{2}, 3\right).$$

Using $\overline{BC}$ as a base, $\triangle ABC$ has base $6 + \frac{3}{2} = \frac{15}{2}$ and height 3 so area

$$\frac{1}{2} \times \frac{15}{2} \times 3 = \frac{45}{4}.$$

As E is the midpoint of $\overline{AC}$, $\triangle ABE$ and $\triangle CBE$ have the same area, so each has area $\frac{45}{4} \div 2 = \frac{45}{8}$. Similarly, D is the midpoint of $\overline{AB}$ so $\triangle ADE$ and $\triangle BDE$ both have area $\frac{45}{8} \div 2 = \frac{45}{16}$. Therefore $P + Q = 45 + 16 = 61$.

Answer: 61

Problem 6 Solution
Note $20 \times 5 = 100$ and $14 \times 7 = 98$ are the largest multiples of 5 and 7 respectively ≤ 100. Thus there are 20 multiples of 5 and 14 multiples of 7 in $1, 2, 3, \ldots, 100$.

However, we do not want multiples of $\text{lcm}(5,7) = 35$. Hence we need to remove 35 and 70. These are counted twice, once for the multiples of 5 and once for the multiples of 7. Therefore there are $20 + 14 - 2 \cdot 2 = 30$ numbers divisible by 5 or 7 but not both.

Answer: 30

Problem 7 Solution
Completing the square on Rick's first answer we have
$$x^2 - 2x + 1 + y^2 + 4y + 4 = 4 + 1 + 4$$
$$(x-1)^2 + (y+2)^2 = 9,$$

so the (wrong) circle has a center of $(1,-2)$ and radius 3. Hence the circle Rick wants has a center of $(1,0)$ with radius 5. This has equation
$$(x-1)^2 + y^2 = 5^2$$
$$x^2 - 2x + 1 + y^2 = 25$$
$$x^2 + y^2 - 2x + 0y = 25.$$
Therefore, $A + B + C = -2 + 0 + 25 = 23$.

Answer: 23

Problem 8 Solution
If the graphs intersect,
$$x^2 + mx + 1 = mx^2 + m \Rightarrow (1-m)x^2 + mx + (1-m) = 0.$$
Using the discriminant we must have
$$m^2 - 4(1-m)(1-m) = m^2 - 4(m^2 - 2m + 1)$$
$$= -3m^2 + 8m - 4$$
$$= (3m-2)(-m+2) \geq 0$$

Therefore $\frac{2}{3} \leq m \leq 2$ so $m = 1$ and $m = 2$ are the only possible integers. Hence our answer (the sum) is $1 + 2 = 3$.

Answer: 3

Problem 9 Solution

You need to buy 3 boxes of cereal. Since the order does not matter and you have 6 choices to choose from, there are $\binom{6}{3} = \frac{6!}{3! \cdot 3!} = 20$ ways to buy the cereal.

There are 3 ways to buy milk (the 3 choices). For the candy bars, there are 5 choices each for you and your sister, so $5 \cdot 5 = 25$ different outcomes.

Multiplying we get a total of $20 \cdot 3 \cdot 25 = 1500$ different collections of groceries.

Answer: 1500

Problem 10 Solution

Distributing we have $y = \frac{1}{16}x^2 + \frac{B}{16}x + \frac{C}{16}$. Note this means we are given the coefficient of x^2.

The parabola has focus $(2,3)$ and horizontal directrix $y = -5$, so the vertex must be $(2,-1)$ as -1 is the average of 3 and -5. Hence our parabola must have equation

$$y+1 = \frac{1}{16}(x-2)^2$$
$$\Rightarrow y+1 = \frac{1}{16}x^2 - \frac{1}{4}x + \frac{1}{4}$$
$$\Rightarrow y = \frac{1}{16}x^2 - \frac{1}{4}x - \frac{3}{4}$$
$$\Rightarrow y = \frac{1}{16}(x^2 - 4x - 12)$$

Therefore $B = -4$.

Answer: -4

Problem 11 Solution

The base has area N^2. If all the edges are of length N, then the four triangular faces are all equilateral triangles, each with area $\dfrac{N^2\sqrt{3}}{4}$. Hence the total surface area is

$$N^2 + 4 \cdot \frac{N^2\sqrt{3}}{4} = N^2(1+\sqrt{3}).$$

As $121 + 121\sqrt{3} = 121(1+\sqrt{3})$ we see $N^2 = 121$ so $N = 11$.

Answer: 11

Problem 12 Solution

To find the last two digits, we only need to keep track of the last two digits when doing calculations. Hence the last two digits of 2009^{2003} are the same as the last two digits of 9^{2003}.

We now look for a pattern in the powers of 9: 9^1, 9^2, 9^3, etc. Remember we only have to keep track of the last two digits.

Power	1	2	3	4	5
9 × Prev.	9	81	729	261	549
Last Two Digits	09	81	29	61	49

It is possible to continue the pattern from here. Alternatively, note that $49^2 = 2401$ has last two digits of 01. Therefore the last two digits of $(9^5)^2 = 9^{10}$ are 01.

This means the powers of 9 have a pattern that repeats every 10 terms, so, for example, the last two digits of 9^{11}, 9^{21}, etc. are all the same as 9^1 which is 09. Similar reasoning tells us the last two digits of 9^{2003} are the same as the last two digits of 9^3 which are 29.

Answer: 29

2.3 ZIML December 2018 Division H

Problem 13 Solution

Starting at the bottom we simplify $2 - \dfrac{2}{1-i}$. We have

$$2 - \frac{2(1+i)}{(1-i)(1+i)} = 2 - \frac{2(1+i)}{2} = 2 - (1+i) = 1-i.$$

Thus after substituting we again have $2 - \dfrac{2}{1-i}$ as the bottom term. Hence we see the pattern continues and at the end we have

$$\frac{2}{1-i} = \frac{2(1+i)}{2} = 1+i.$$

Hence $A^2 + B^2 = 1^2 + 1^2 = 2$.

Answer: 2

Problem 14 Solution

As all the angles of the octagon are equal, each interior angle has measure $\dfrac{180°(8-2)}{8} = 135°$. Hence all the external angles are $180° - 135° = 45°$ and adding 45-45-90 triangles to the sides of the octagon gives the rectangle shown below.

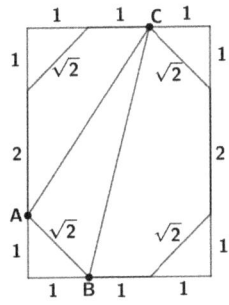

Therefore using the Pythagorean theorem we have

$$AC = \sqrt{3^2 + 2^2} = \sqrt{13} \text{ and } BC = \sqrt{1^2 + 4^2} = \sqrt{17}.$$

Thus the Law of Cosines says

$$AC^2 = AB^2 + BC^2 - 2 \cdot AB \cdot BC \cdot \cos \angle ABC$$
$$13 = 2 + 17 - 2 \cdot \sqrt{2} \cdot \sqrt{17} \cdot \cos \angle ABC$$
$$13 = 19 - 2\sqrt{34} \cdot \cos \angle ABC.$$

Therefore $\cos \angle ABC = \dfrac{-6}{-2\sqrt{34}} = \dfrac{3\sqrt{34}}{34}$ when written in simplest radical form and $P + Q + R = 3 + 34 + 34 = 71$.

Answer: 71

Problem 15 Solution

To find the overall probability, we add the different cases together:

$$20\% \cdot 50\% + 50\% \cdot 80\% + 30\% \cdot 90\%$$
$$= 0.2 \cdot 0.5 + 0.5 \cdot 0.8 + 0.3 \cdot 0.9$$
$$= 0.1 + 0.4 + 0.27$$
$$= 0.77$$

As $0.77 = 77\%$, $K = 77$.

Answer: 77

Problem 16 Solution

We know $\sin \angle ABD = \frac{4}{5}$. Since $AD = 4$ and $AB = 5$, this means that $\triangle ABD$ is a right triangle. Thus $BD = 3$ using the Pythagorean theorem.

Now $\triangle BCD$ is also right, so

$$\sin \angle ACB = \sin \angle DCB = \frac{BD}{BC} = \frac{5}{7}.$$

Hence $BC = BD \div \left(\dfrac{5}{7}\right) = \dfrac{21}{5}$. As a decimal $\dfrac{21}{5} = 4.2$ which is our answer.

Answer: 4.2

2.3 ZIML December 2018 Division H

Problem 17 Solution

Using the sine addition formula we have

$$\sin(2\theta + 30°) = \sin(2\theta)\cos(30°) + \cos(2\theta)\sin(30°)$$
$$= \frac{\sqrt{3}}{2}\sin(2\theta) + \frac{1}{2}\cos(2\theta).$$

Thus substituting our equation becomes

$$\sqrt{3}\sin(2\theta) + \cos(2\theta) = \cos(2\theta) + \sqrt{3}$$

and hence $\sin(2\theta) = 1$. Therefore, $2\theta = 90°, 450°, \ldots$ and $\theta = 45°, 225°, \ldots$. We want the smallest $\theta > 180°$, so $\theta = 225$.

Answer: 225

Problem 18 Solution

The prime factorization of 1000 is $2^3 \cdot 5^3$. This means that 1000 has $(3+1)(3+1) = 16$ factors. Note these factors can be paired up (1 and 1000, 2 and 500, etc.) so that each factor pair multiplies to 1000.

Thus there are $16 \div 2 = 8$ factor pairs and hence the product of the factors is
$$1000^8 = (10^3)^8 = 10^{24}.$$

Therefore $K = 24$ is the answer.

Answer: 24

Problem 19 Solution

Extending the sides of the trapezoid we create a large triangle, as shown below.

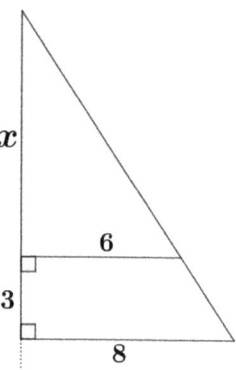

We first find the missing value x using similar triangles:

$$\frac{x}{6} = \frac{x+3}{8} \Rightarrow 8x = 6x + 18 \Rightarrow x = 9.$$

The solid created when rotating the trapezoid is called a frustrum or a truncated cone. This is a cone with its top (another cone) removed. In this case the full cone has radius 8 with height $9 + 3 = 12$ so its volume is

$$\frac{1}{3} \times \pi \times 8^2 \times 12 = 256\pi.$$

The top cone has radius 6 and height 9 and thus volume

$$\frac{1}{3} \times \pi \times 6^2 \times 9 = 108\pi.$$

Hence the solid has volume $256\pi - 108\pi = 148\pi$ and $K = 148$.

Answer: 148

2.3 ZIML December 2018 Division H

Problem 20 Solution

First note if $x = 1 - i$ is a solution, then so is its conjugate $1 + i$. By the factor theorem, we therefore know that $(x-1)$, $(x-(1-i))$ and $(x-(1+i))$ are all factors of $x^3 + Ax^2 + Bx + C$. Thus

$$x^3 + Ax^2 + Bx + C = (x-1)(x-(1-i))(x-(1+i)).$$

We want C, so multiplying out the constant terms we have

$$C = -(1-i)(1+i) = -2.$$

Answer: -2

2.4 ZIML January 2019 Division H

Below are the solutions from the Division H ZIML Competition held in January 2019.
The problems from the contest are available on p.41.

Problem 1 Solution
First note that as $\angle C = 100°$ we must have $AD = BD$ in isosceles triangle $\triangle ABD$.

Therefore, if $x = \angle A = \angle BAD$ we have $\angle ABD = x$ and hence $\angle ABC = 2x$ as $\overline{BD}$ bisects $\angle B$. Thus

$$\begin{aligned} 180 &= \angle A + \angle B + \angle C \\ &= x + 2x + 100 \\ &= 3x + 100 \end{aligned}$$

so $3x = 80$ and $x = \dfrac{80}{3} = 26.\overline{6}$. Rounded to the nearest tenth we have $x \approx 26.7$.

Answer: 26.7

Problem 2 Solution
Two volunteers are needed each for Friday, Saturday, and Sunday. As students are not chosen twice, there are thus

$$\binom{11}{2} \cdot \binom{9}{2} \cdot \binom{7}{2} = \frac{11 \cdot 10 \cdot 9 \cdot 8 \cdot 7 \cdot 6}{2 \cdot 2 \cdot 2} = 41580,$$

ways to choose the groups to volunteer.

(We use combinations because the order of the volunteers does not matter each day.)

Answer: 41580

2.4 ZIML January 2019 Division H

Problem 3 Solution

There are many ways to find the prime factorization. One trick is noticing the following:

$$222222 = 1001 \times 222,$$

so we are left to factor 1001 and 222. $1001 = 7 \times 11 \times 13$ while $222 = 2 \times 3 \times 37$. Hence the prime factors of $222,222$ are 2, 3, 7, 11, 13, and 37, with sum 73.

Answer: 73

Problem 4 Solution

The slope from A to B is

$$\frac{6-3}{4-(-2)} = \frac{3}{6} = \frac{1}{2},$$

so the perpendicular bisector has slope -2. The midpoint of $\overline{AB}$ is

$$\left(\frac{-2+4}{2}, \frac{3+6}{2}\right) = (1, 4.5).$$

Therefore, the equation for the perpendicular bisector is

$$y - \frac{9}{2} = -2(x-1) \Rightarrow y = -2x + 6.5.$$

Solving the x-intercept is $6.5 \div 2 = 3.25$.

Answer: 3.25

Problem 5 Solution

First consider $x^2 + 4x - 2 = 2$ so $x^2 + 4x - 4 = 0$. Using the quadratic formula we have solutions of

$$\frac{-4 \pm \sqrt{4^2 - 4 \times -4}}{2} = -2 \pm 2\sqrt{2}.$$

The other case is $x^2+4x-2 = -2$ so $x^2+4x = 0$. Factoring this gives solutions of $x = 0$ and $x = -4$.

Note $\sqrt{2} > 1$, so $-2-2\sqrt{2} < -4$, so it is the smallest solution. Similarly $-2+2\sqrt{2} > 0$ so it is the largest solution. Thus the sum of these solutions is

$$-2-2\sqrt{2} + -2+2\sqrt{2} = -4,$$

which gives our answer.

Answer: -4

Problem 6 Solution
Let arcs $\widehat{AC} = x$ and $\widehat{BD} = y$. Then

$$\angle AEC = 20° = \frac{1}{2}(\widehat{AC} - \widehat{BD}) = \frac{1}{2}(x-y)$$

and also

$$180° = \widehat{AC} + \widehat{CD} + \widehat{BD} = x + y + 80°.$$

Thus we have the system of equations

$$x - y = 40 \text{ and } x + y = 100.$$

Solving we get $x = 70$ and $y = 30$. Therefore $\widehat{AC} = 70°$ and thus inscribed angle $\angle ABC$ has measure $\widehat{AC} \div 2 = 70° \div 2 = 35°$.

Answer: 35

Problem 7 Solution
Let $z = \sqrt{x^2+x+2}$ so the equation becomes $z + z^2 = 6$ so factoring we have

$$z^2 + z - 6 = (z+3)(z-2) = 0$$

and hence $z = -3$ or $z = 2$. Square roots are always non-negative, so $z = -3$ is impossible, therefore $\sqrt{x^2 + x + 2} = 2$. Squaring and solving we have

$$x^2 + x - 2 = (x+2)(x-1) = 0$$

so the roots are $x = -2$ and $x = 1$. Thus $A - B = 1 - (-2) = 3$.

Answer: 3

Problem 8 Solution
Since the area of $\triangle CDE$ is 27, it has height h_1 with

$$\frac{1}{2} \times h_1 \times CD = \frac{1}{2} \times h_1 \times 9 = 27$$

and hence $h_1 = 27 \times 2 \div 9 = 6$.

$AB \| CD$, so $\triangle CDE$ is similar to $\triangle ABE$ with ratio of sides $9 : 6 = 3 : 2$. Hence their heights are also in ratio $3 : 2$ so the height h_2 of $\triangle ABE$ satisfies

$$3 : 2 = h_1 : h_2 = 6 : h_2 \Rightarrow h_2 = 4.$$

Therefore the height of the trapezoid is $h_1 + h_2 = 6 + 4 = 10$.

Answer: 10

Problem 9 Solution
First assume one of the knights is in the center square. In this case the second knight can be in any of the 8 remaining squares, giving 8 total possibilities.

Now assume both knights are in the outer 8 squares. Notice that if one knight is in any of the 8 positions, it can move to exactly 2 others. Hence there are

$$8 \times (7 - 2) \div 2 = 20$$

outcomes where both knights are in the outer squares. We must divide by 2 because the rooks are identical to avoid overcounting.

Thus there are $20 + 8 = 28$ arrangements.

Answer: 28

Problem 10 Solution

Let l, w, and h denote the length, width, and height of the original prism.

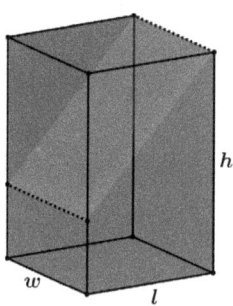

Considering top volume, we have a triangular prism. The base of this prism is a triangle with dimensions l and $\frac{2}{3}h$ (as the plane is cut $\frac{1}{3}$ up the side) and the height is w. Hence it has volume

$$\frac{1}{2} \cdot l \cdot \frac{2}{3}h \cdot w = \frac{1}{3}lwh.$$

Note this is $\frac{1}{3}$ of the entire volume, hence the ratio of the volumes of the two pieces is

$$\frac{1}{3} : \frac{2}{3} = 1 : 2$$

and $P^2 + Q^2 = 1^2 + 2^2 = 5$.

Answer: 5

2.4 ZIML January 2019 Division H

Problem 11 Solution

The vertex of parabola $y = ax^2 + bx + c$ has x-coordinate $x = -\dfrac{b}{2a}$.

Thus the vertex of $y = x^2 + 5x + 6$ has x-coordinate $-\dfrac{6}{2} = -3$.
Hence the y-coordinate of its vertex is

$$(-3)^2 + 6(-3) + 5 = -4.$$

Similarly for the coordinates of the vertex of $y = -x^2 + 10x - 23$ we have

$$x = -\dfrac{10}{-2} = 5,$$
$$\text{and } y = -(5)^2 + 10(5) - 23 = 2.$$

Therefore we want the distance from $(-3, -4)$ to $(5, 2)$ which is

$$\sqrt{(5-(-3))^2 + (2-(-4))^2} = \sqrt{64 + 36} = \sqrt{100},$$

and thus $M = 100$.

Answer: 100

Problem 12 Solution

Since a and b are the roots of the same quadratic equation, they must be conjugates. Therefore

$$a, b = R \pm iS$$

for real numbers R and S. We are given that $S = 3$. Further

$$2R = (R + iS) + (R - iS) = a + b = \dfrac{4}{3}$$
$$\Rightarrow R = \dfrac{2}{3}$$

Thus
$$a \times b = \left(\frac{2}{3} + 3i\right)\left(\frac{2}{3} - 3i\right)$$
$$= \frac{4}{9} - 9i^2$$
$$= \frac{4}{9} + 9$$
$$= \frac{85}{9}.$$

Hence $P + Q = 85 + 9 = 94$.

Answer: 94

Problem 13 Solution

Since we know $AB = 2$ and $BC = 8$, given $\cos(\angle B)$ we can calculate AC^2 using the Law of Cosines.

To find $\cos(\angle B)$ using the Law of Cosines for $\triangle ABD$.

$$16 = AD^2 = AB^2 + BD^2 - 2 \cdot AB \cdot BD \cdot \cos(\angle B)$$
$$= 4 + 25 - 20\cos(\angle B)$$

and thus $\cos(\angle B) = \dfrac{13}{20}$. Therefore

$$AC^2 = AB^2 + BC^2 - 2 \cdot AB \cdot BC \cdot \cos(\angle B)$$
$$= 4 + 64 - 32 \cdot \frac{13}{20}$$
$$= 68 - \frac{104}{5}$$
$$= \frac{236}{5}.$$

Hence $P + Q = 236 + 5 = 241$.

Answer: 241

Problem 14 Solution
Using the change of base formula
$$\log_x(16) = \frac{\log_4(16)}{\log_4(x)} = \frac{2}{\log_4(x)}$$
so after the substitution $y = \log_4(x)$ we have
$$y + \frac{2}{y} = \frac{9}{2}.$$
Clearing denominators we get $2y^2 + 4 = 9y$ or $2y^2 - 9y + 4 = 0$. Factoring gives
$$2y^2 - 9y + 4 = (2y - 1)(y - 4) = 0.$$
Therefore $y = \frac{1}{2}$ or $y = 4$ and hence $x = 4^{1/2} = 2$ or $x = 4^4 = 256$. The sum of these two solutions is thus $2 + 256 = 258$.

Answer: 258

Problem 15 Solution
We know the area of $\triangle ABC$ is given by
$$\frac{1}{2} \cdot AB \cdot BC \cdot \sin \angle ABC = \frac{1}{2} \cdot AB \cdot 6 \cdot \sin 45°$$
$$= AB \cdot \frac{3\sqrt{2}}{2}.$$
We know $AB > BC = 6$. Hence
$$K = AB \cdot \frac{3\sqrt{2}}{2} > 6 \cdot \frac{3\sqrt{2}}{2} = 9\sqrt{2}.$$
As $9\sqrt{2} = \sqrt{162}$ we know
$$K > \sqrt{162} > \sqrt{144} = 12$$
and therefore the smallest possible value of K is 13.

Answer: 13

Problem 16 Solution

Eric arrives randomly within a 1 hour time-span while Morgan arrives randomly within a 1.5 hour time-span. Therefore we can plot all the arrivals within the 2×3 grid shown below (each square is 0.5 hours by 0.5 hours).

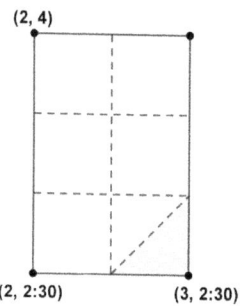

The shaded triangle represents when Eric arrives before Morgan (the x-coordinate is greater than the y-coordinate). Thus the probability is $\dfrac{1}{12} = 0.08\overline{3} = 8.\overline{3}\%$. K rounded to the nearest integer is 8.

Answer: 8

Problem 17 Solution

Let N be an integer ≥ 1. Then $N^2 + 1 < (N+1)^2$ so

$$N < \sqrt{N^2+1} < N+1.$$

Therefore if n is even we have

$$\begin{aligned}
a_n &= \left\lfloor (-1)^n \sqrt{(a_{n-1})^2 + 1} \right\rfloor \\
&= \left\lfloor \sqrt{(a_{n-1})^2 + 1} \right\rfloor \\
&= |a_{n-1}|.
\end{aligned}$$

2.4 ZIML January 2019 Division H

If n is odd we have
$$a_n = \left\lfloor (-1)^n \sqrt{(a_{n-1})^2 + 1} \right\rfloor$$
$$= \left\lfloor (-1) \sqrt{(a_{n-1})^2 + 1} \right\rfloor$$
$$= -|a_{n-1}| - 1.$$

Thus our sequence starts
$$4, -5, 5, -6, 6, -7, 7, \ldots$$
and we notice $a_0, a_2, a_4, \ldots$ equals
$$4, 5, 6, \ldots.$$
Therefore $a_{20} = 4 + 20 \div 2 = 14$.

Answer: 14

Problem 18 Solution

Solving the first equation for x^2 we have $x^2 = y + 4$. Substituting we have
$$y + 4 + y^2 = 4 \Rightarrow y(y+1) = 0$$
so $y = 0$ or $y = -1$. Solving for x in each case we have
$$y = 0 \Rightarrow x^2 = 4 \Rightarrow x = \pm 2$$
$$y = -1 \Rightarrow x^2 = 3 \Rightarrow x = \pm\sqrt{3}$$
Hence the 4 vertices of the quadrilateral have coordinates
$$(-2, 0), (2, 0), (-\sqrt{3}, -1), (\sqrt{3}, -1).$$
Thus this is a trapezoid with bases of length 4 and $2\sqrt{3}$ with height 1. Therefore the area is
$$\frac{4 + 2\sqrt{3}}{2} \times 1 = 2 + \sqrt{3},$$
so $A + B + C = 2 + 1 + 3 = 6$.

Answer: 6

Problem 19 Solution

$99 = 9 \times 11$ so we need the number to be divisible by 9 and by 11.

To be divisible by 9 we need the sum of the digits to be divisible by 9, so

$$2+0+a+b+1+a+9 = 2a+b+12$$

must be divisible by 9.

To be divisible by 11 we need the alternating sum of the digits to be divisible by 11, so

$$9-a+1-b+a-0+2 = 12-b$$

must be divisible by 11. From this equation, we see (since b is a digit) that $b = 1$.

Plugging into the first equation, $2a+1+12 = 2a+13$ must be a multiple of 9, so

$$2a+13 = 18, 27, 36, \ldots.$$

Again a is a digit, so we must have $2a+13 = 27$ so $a = 7$.

This gives $10a+b = 70+1 = 71$.

Answer: 71

Problem 20 Solution

Clearing denominators we have

$$2\sin(2x)\cos(2x) = \sqrt{3}\cos(4x).$$

Using the double-angle formula, the left-hand side is

$$2\sin(2x)\cos(2x) = \sin(4x).$$

Hence dividing by $\cos(4x)$ we get

$$\frac{\sin(4x)}{\cos(4x)} = \tan(4x) = \sqrt{3}.$$

Since $\tan^{-1}(\sqrt{3}) = 60°$ we have

$$4x = 60°, 240°, 420°, 600°, 780°, \ldots$$
$$\text{and thus } x = 15°, 60°, 105°, 150°, 195°, \ldots$$

The sum of all solutions from $0°$ to $180°$ is

$$15° + 60° + 105° + 150° = 330°$$

so the answer is 330.

Answer: 330

2.5 ZIML February 2019 Division H

Below are the solutions from the Division H ZIML Competition held in February 2019.
The problems from the contest are available on p.47.

Problem 1 Solution
Label the three equations (i), (ii), and (iii). Then $(i) - (ii) + (iii)$ gives
$$3z = 6 \Rightarrow z = 2.$$
Plugging this into (iii),
$$y + 2 \cdot 2 = 5 \Rightarrow y = 1.$$
Finally, using (i) we have
$$x + 2 \cdot 1 + 3 \cdot 2 = 9 \Rightarrow x = 1.$$
Hence
$$x^2 + y^2 + z^2 = 1^2 + 1^2 + 2^2 = 6$$
is our answer.

Answer: 6

Problem 2 Solution
In total there are $6^3 = 216$ outcomes. We consider 6 cases based on the first roll.

If the first roll is 1 or 2, it is impossible for the sum of the last two rolls to be less than the first.

If the first roll is 3, the second and third must sum to 2, which gives 1 outcome for the last two rolls: $(1,1)$.

If the first roll is 4, the second and third can additionally sum to 3, which gives 2 additional outcomes for the last two rolls: $(2,1), (1,2)$. Hence there are $1 + 2 = 3$ outcomes here.

Following the pattern we get the results below:

1st Roll	# of Outcomes for Last Two Rolls
1	0
2	0
3	1
4	3
5	6
6	10

Therefore there are $1+3+6+10 = 20$ outcomes where the sum of the last two rolls is less than the first roll. This gives a probability of
$$\frac{20}{6^3} = \frac{20}{216} = \frac{5}{54},$$
and $Q - P = 54 - 5 = 49$.

Answer: 49

Problem 3 Solution

Since we want only the last digit, we can ignore the other digits. We first find the last digits of 2^{100} and 9^{100} using patterns.

Looking at the last digit of $2^1, 2^2, 2^3, \ldots$ we have
$$2, 4, 8, 6, 2, 4, 8, 6, \ldots$$
so we see the pattern repeats every four terms. 100 is a multiple of 4, so 2^{100} has last digit 6.

Proceeding similarly with powers of 9, $9^1, 9^2, \ldots$ we have
$$9, 1, 9, 1, \ldots$$
where the pattern repeats every two terms. 100 is even, so 9^{100} has last digit 1.

Adding we see $2^{100} + 19^{100}$ has last digit $6 + 1 = 7$.

Answer: 7

Problem 4 Solution

We know there is 1 of the 4 face cards and it can be in any of the 5 spots. Thus there are 20 different ways to place the face card.

The four remaining spots are filled (in order) with 4 of the 9 numbered cards. Since we already know their order, we just need to decide which of the 4 cards to choose, which can be done in

$$\binom{9}{4} = \frac{9 \cdot 8 \cdot 7 \cdot 6}{4 \cdot 3 \cdot 2 \cdot 1} = 126$$

ways. In total we thus have $20 \cdot 126 = 2520$ outcomes.

Answer: 2520

Problem 5 Solution

Consider the diagram below

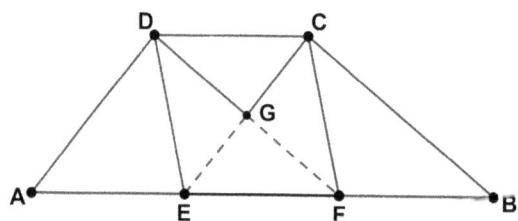

As $\overline{AB} \parallel \overline{CD}$ with $CD = AE = EF = BF$, $\triangle ADE$, $\triangle CED$, $\triangle ECF$, and $\triangle BFC$ all have the same base and same height, so each are $\frac{1}{4}$ of the trapezoid.

Hence $CDEF$ is half the trapezoid. Further, $CDEF$ is a trapezoid with equal bases ($CD = EF$) so $CDEF$ is a parallelogram. This implies that $\triangle CDG$, $\triangle DEG$, $\triangle EFG$, and $\triangle FCG$ all are equal area. Therefore we see that the area of $EFCGD$ is

$$\frac{1}{2} \cdot \frac{3}{4} = \frac{3}{8} = 0.375$$

2.5 ZIML February 2019 Division H

of the entire trapezoid. Hence $K = 37.5$.

Answer: 37.5

Problem 6 Solution

We know a regular polygon with n sides has interior angles of $\dfrac{180°(n-2)}{n}$. Therefore a pentagon (5 sides), hexagon (6 sides), octagon (8 sides), and decagon (10 sides) have respectively interior angles of

$$108°, 120°, 135°, \text{ and } 144°.$$

Starting in the upper-right and proceeding clockwise, we get the four angles measure

$$360° - 90° - 108° - 135° = 27°$$
$$360° - 90° - 135° - 120° = 15°$$
$$360° - 90° - 120° - 144° = 6°$$
$$360° - 90° - 144° - 108° = 18°.$$

Adding we get an answer of $27 + 15 + 6 + 18 = 66$.

Answer: 66

Problem 7 Solution

Since $c = 1 + 2i$ we have

$$c^2 = (1 + 2i)^2$$
$$= 1 + 4i + 4i^2$$
$$= -3 + 4i.$$

Hence multiplying by the conjugate $-3 - 4i$ we have

$$\frac{1}{c^2} = \frac{-3 - 4i}{(-3 + 4i)(-3 - 4i)}$$
$$= \frac{-3 - 4i}{9 - 4i^2}$$
$$= \frac{-3 - 4i}{25}.$$

Adding we thus have
$$c^2 + \frac{1}{c^2} = \frac{25(-3+4i)}{25} + \frac{-3-4i}{25}$$
$$= \frac{-75+100i-3-4i}{25}$$
$$= -\frac{78}{25} + \frac{96}{25}i.$$

Therefore the imaginary part is $\frac{96}{25}$ and $P+Q = 96+25 = 121$.

Answer: 121

Problem 8 Solution

Continuing the pattern we get the next few terms are
$$i, -1, 0, 0, 1, i, \ldots.$$
Note that the sequence has started repeating, so the sequence repeats the 8 terms
$$1, i, i+1, i-1, i, -1, 0, 0, \ldots$$
over and over. Therefore the 1st, 9th, 17th, etc. terms are all the start of the pattern. Thus the 97th term is 1 and hence we can find the hundredth term to be $i-1 = -1+i$. Therefore $2A+3B = 2(-1)+3(1) = 1$.

Answer: 1

Problem 9 Solution

Using the discriminant Δ we have
$$\Delta = 8^2 - 4 \cdot 2k \cdot k = 64 - 8k^2.$$
For the quadratic to have two real roots we need $\Delta > 0$. Hence
$$64 - 8k^2 > 0$$
$$8k^2 < 64$$
$$k^2 < 8$$

2.5 ZIML February 2019 Division H

Therefore we have integer values of ± 2, ± 1, and 0. However, when $k = 0$ our equation is the line $y = 8x$, which only has one solution. Hence there are 4 integer values of k that work.

Answer: 4

Problem 10 Solution
We first find the prime factorization of 430848. Using divisibility rules we easily see it is divisible by 8, 9, and 11. Hence we can factor
$$430848 = 2^3 \cdot 3^2 \cdot 11 \cdot 544$$
so after factoring $544 = 2^5 \cdot 17$ we have
$$430848 = 2^8 \cdot 3^2 \cdot 11 \cdot 17.$$
This is not a perfect square, as the exponents of 11 and 17 are not even. Hence $N = 2^8 \cdot 3^2 \cdot 11^2 \cdot 17^2$ will be the smallest perfect square that is a multiple of N. This number has
$$(8+1)(2+1)(2+1)(2+1) = 9 \cdot 3^3 = 243$$
factors.

Answer: 243

Problem 11 Solution
Let the smallest side be x. Then for a common difference $d > 0$, we must have that the sides are x, $x+d$, and $x+2d$. Using the Pythagorean theorem
$$x^2 + (x+d)^2 = (x+2d)^2$$
$$x^2 + x^2 + 2dx + d^2 = x^2 + 4dx + 4d^2$$
$$x^2 - 2dx - 3d^2 = 0$$
$$(x - 3d)(x + d) = 0$$
Hence either $x = 3d$ or $x = -d$. Since $d > 0$, $x = -d$ is impossible so $x = 3d$. Therefore the sides of the triangle are $3d$, $4d$, and $5d$.

Solving for d (using the area) we have

$$\frac{1}{2} \cdot 3d \cdot 4d = 96$$
$$6d^2 = 96$$
$$d^2 = 16$$
$$d = \pm 4.$$

Again, $d > 0$ so $d = 4$. Hence the smallest side is $3d = 3 \cdot 4 = 12$.

Answer: 12

Problem 12 Solution

The original cube has a surface area of $6 \cdot 4^2 = 96$.

Peter cuts out 6 cubes with side length 1 inch. For each of these, we are removing the surface area from one face (where the cube is cut out of the 4 inch cube) but adding 5 faces. Therefore we add an extra surface area of

$$6 \cdot (5 - 1) \cdot 1^2 = 24.$$

Hence the total surface area is $96 + 24 = 120$.

Answer: 120

Problem 13 Solution

Connect A, B, and C to the center of the circle as shown.

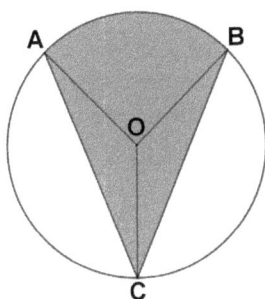

First note sector AOB is a quarter circle, hence has area

$$\frac{1}{4} \cdot \pi \cdot 6^2 = 9\pi.$$

Since $AC = BC$ the measures of $\widehat{AC}$ and $\widehat{BC}$ are the same. Hence both measure

$$\frac{360° - 90°}{2} = 135°.$$

$\triangle AOC \cong \triangle BOC$ and both have two sides of length 6 with an angle of $135°$. Thus each has area

$$\frac{1}{2} \cdot 6 \cdot 6 \cdot \sin(135°) = 18 \cdot \frac{\sqrt{2}}{2} = 9\sqrt{2}.$$

Therefore the entire area is

$$9\pi + 2 \cdot 9\sqrt{2} = 9\pi + 18\sqrt{2}$$

and $A + B + C = 9 + 18 + 2 = 29$.

Answer: 29

Problem 14 Solution
The circles have equations

$$(x-3)^2 + y^2 = 5^2 \Rightarrow x^2 - 6x + y^2 = 16$$
$$(x+7)^2 + (y-5)^2 = (5\sqrt{2})^2 \Rightarrow x^2 + 14x + y^2 - 10y = -24$$

Subtracting the two equations we have $-20x + 10y = 40$ or $y = 2x + 4$. Substituting into the first equation we have

$$x^2 - 6x + (2x+4)^2 = 16$$
$$5x^2 + 10x = 0$$
$$5x(x+2) = 0$$

and hence $x = 0$ or $x = -2$. This gives $y = 4$ and $y = 0$ respectively. Therefore the midpoint is

$$\left(\frac{0+(-2)}{2}, \frac{4+0}{2}\right) = (-1, 2)$$

so $M + N = -1 + 2 = 1$.

Answer: 1

Problem 15 Solution
Letting $z = x^2$ we have

$$z^2 - 9z + 20 = (z-5)(z-4) = 0$$

and hence $z = x^2 = 5$ or $z = x^2 = 4$. Therefore the only integer solutions are ± 2 with product -4.

Answer: -4

Problem 16 Solution
Let O be the origin. Using the distance formula

$$OA = \sqrt{3^2 + 1^2} = \sqrt{10}.$$

ZOOM INTERNATIONAL MATH LEAGUE: ziml.areteem.org

2.5 ZIML February 2019 Division H

Therefore $OB = \sqrt{10}$ as well. Thus $\triangle AOB$ is isosceles with two sides of $\sqrt{10}$ with an angle of $30°$. Using the Law of Cosines we have

$$\begin{aligned} D^2 = AB^2 &= OA^2 + OB^2 - 2 \cdot OA \cdot OB \cdot \cos(\angle AOB) \\ &= 10 + 10 - 2 \cdot 10 \cdot \cos(30°) \\ &= 20 - 10\sqrt{3} \\ &\approx 20 - 10 \cdot 1.73 \\ &= 20 - 17.3 \\ &= 2.7 \end{aligned}$$

Therefore $D^2 \approx 2.7$ is our answer.

Answer: 2.7

Problem 17 Solution

If $y = L$ then

$$L = 2x, L = 4x, L = 6x, \text{ and } L = 8x$$

for the four lines. Hence each of

$$x = \frac{L}{2}, x = \frac{L}{4}, x = \frac{L}{6}, \text{ and } x = \frac{L}{8}$$

must be integers. Therefore the smallest value of L is

$$\text{lcm}(2,4,6,8) = \text{lcm}(6,8) = 24,$$

which is our answer.

Answer: 24

Problem 18 Solution

The minimum value of $y = x^2 - 6x + 13$ occurs when $x = -\frac{-6}{2} = 3$. Hence the minimum is $3^2 - 6 \cdot 3 + 13 = 4$.

Similar the maximum value of $y = -x^2 - 2x + P$ occurs when $x = -\frac{-2}{-2} = -1$. Since the minimum value must be 4, we get

$$4 = -(-1)^2 - 2(-1) + P = 1 + P.$$

Solving for P we have $P = 3$.

Answer: 3

Problem 19 Solution
For the product to equal 0, one of the terms must equal 0. Since $\cos(90°) = 0$ we can have

$$x, 2x, 3x, 4x = 90°,$$

Hence $x = 90, 45, 30,$ and $22.5°$ all work. However, $\cos(90° + N \cdot 180°) = 0$ for all integers N. Hence we can also have

$$x, 2x, 3x, 4x = 270°, 450°, \text{ or } 630°$$

which give $x = 270$, $x = 135$, $x = 90$, and $x = 67.5$, or $x = 450$, $x = 225$, $x = 150$, and $x = 112.5$, or $x = 630$, $x = 315$, $x = 210$, and $x = 157.5$.

Only 67.5, 112.5, 135, 150, and 157.5 are in the range we want.

No other values of $90° + N \cdot 180°$ work, so the sum of the solutions in the given range is

$$90 + 45 + 30 + 22.5 + 67.5 + 112.5 + 135 + 150 + 157.5 = 810,$$

which gives our answer.

Answer: 810

2.5 ZIML February 2019 Division H

Problem 20 Solution

If $f(3) = k$ then $f^{-1}(k) = 3$. Therefore we want k so that $\log_2(4k-1) = 3$. Solving for k we have

$$4k - 1 = 2^3$$
$$4k = 8 + 1$$
$$k = \frac{9}{4}$$

Thus $f(3) = \frac{9}{4}$ and $P + Q = 9 + 4 = 13$.

Answer: 13

2.6 ZIML March 2019 Division H

Below are the solutions from the Division H ZIML Competition held in March 2019.
The problems from the contest are available on p.55.

Problem 1 Solution

Since $\tan(\theta) = \dfrac{\sin(\theta)}{\cos(\theta)}$, cross multiplying we have

$$\tan(\theta) = \sin(\theta) \Rightarrow \sin(\theta) = \sin(\theta)\cos(\theta)$$

as long as $\cos(\theta) \neq 0$. Therefore both equations have the same solutions unless $\cos(\theta) = 0$.

Factoring this equation we get

$$\sin(\theta)(\cos(\theta) - 1) = 0$$

so $\sin(\theta) = 0$ or $\cos(\theta) = 1$. Therefore we have solutions of $\theta = 0°$ (giving $\sin(\theta) = 0$ and $\cos(\theta) = 1$) and $\theta = 180°$ (giving $\sin(\theta) = 0$ and $\cos(\theta) = -1$). Thus there are 2 solutions in common.

Answer: 2

Problem 2 Solution

The angles in a pentagon add up to $180°(5-2) = 540°$. Let x denote the measure of the each of the congruent angles. Then the fourth and fifth angles measure $x + 20$ and $x - 80$ degrees respectively. Hence

$$x + x + x + (x + 20) + (x - 80) = 540.$$

Solving we have $5x - 60 = 540$ so $x = 600 \div 5 = 120$, which is our answer.

Answer: 120

ZOOM INTERNATIONAL MATH LEAGUE: ziml.areteem.org

Problem 3 Solution

First choose which action figures Stan will line up. There are

$$\binom{5}{3} \cdot \binom{6}{3} = \frac{5 \cdot 4}{2} \cdot \frac{6 \cdot 5 \cdot 4}{6} = 200$$

ways to choose 3 of each type of action figure. Once they are chosen, Stan needs to line up the 6 action figures. Choosing place by place there are $6! = 720$ ways to line them up. This gives

$$200 \cdot 720 = 144000$$

total arrangements.

Answer: 144000

Problem 4 Solution

As we start with a square, the two inner shapes shown in the diagram are each parallelograms.

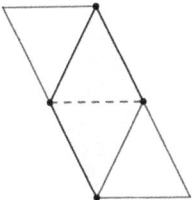

Dividing the larger parallelogram, we see it has twice the area of the shaded region, so this larger parallelogram has area $2 \cdot 16 = 32$. Identical reasoning gives that the full square has twice the area of this parallelogram: $2 \cdot 32 = 64$.

Answer: 64

Problem 5 Solution

Make the substitution $u = \sqrt{x}$, so that our function becomes

$$y = -u^2 + 4u + 12.$$

This quadratic has a maximum when $u = -\dfrac{4}{-2} = 2$. Therefore our graph has a maximum when $\sqrt{x} = 2$ so $x = 4$. This maximum is

$$-4 + 4\sqrt{4} + 12 = 16.$$

Thus $R + S = 4 + 16 = 20$.

Answer: 20

Problem 6 Solution

Looking at a table of values of possible scores with 0 touchdowns, 1 touchdown, and 2 touchdowns we have

Num. Touchdowns	Possible Scores
0	$0, 3, 6, 9, 12, 15, \ldots$
1	$7, 10, 13, 16, \ldots$
2	$14, 17, 20, \ldots$

From this list it is clear that

$$1, 2, 4, 5, 8, \text{ and } 11$$

are all impossible scores. Further we see $12, 15, 18, \ldots$ are all possible with 0 touchdowns, $13, 16, 19, \ldots$ are all possible with 1 touchdown, and $14, 17, 20, \ldots$ are all possible with 2 touchdowns. With this pattern all scores ≥ 12 are possible.

Hence of the 51 scores from 0 to 50, only 6 are impossible, meaning $51 - 6 = 45$ difference scores as possible.

Answer: 45

2.6 ZIML March 2019 Division H

Problem 7 Solution
Using rules of exponents and logarithms,

$$\log\left(\frac{100\sqrt{M^3}}{N^2}\right)$$
$$= \log\left(\frac{100M^{3/2}}{N^2}\right)$$
$$= \log(100) + \log(M^{3/2}) - \log(N^2)$$
$$= 2 + \frac{3}{2}\log(M) - 2\log(N)$$
$$= 2 + \frac{3}{2} \cdot 1.5 - 2 \cdot (-0.2)$$
$$= 2 + 2.25 + 0.4$$
$$= 4.65$$

which is our answer.

Answer: 4.65

Problem 8 Solution
Calculating the missing angles we have $\angle B = 105°$ and $\angle F = 30°$. Therefore the two triangles are similar with $\triangle ABC \sim \triangle FED$.

Using the Law of Sines on $\triangle ABC$ we have

$$\frac{\sin \angle A}{BC} = \frac{\sin \angle C}{AB}$$
$$AB \sin 30° = BC \sin 45°$$
$$5\sqrt{2} \cdot \frac{1}{2} = BC \cdot \frac{\sqrt{2}}{2}$$

so $BC = 5$. This side corresponds to side $DE = 3$ in $\triangle DEF$, so the ratio of areas is the same as the square of the ratio of sides (since the triangles are similar). Hence

$$R = \frac{BC^2}{DE^2} = \frac{25}{9} \approx 2.777,$$

so rounded to the nearest tenth R is 2.8.

Answer: 2.8

Problem 9 Solution

Filling in the missing data from the chart we have

	Red	Yellow	Total
Boys	22	18	40
Girls	32	12	44
Total	54	30	84

Since 54 students preferred red and 32 were girls, the probability is
$$\frac{32}{54} = \frac{16}{27}$$
so $P + Q = 16 + 27 = 43$.

Answer: 43

Problem 10 Solution

Let c denote the height of Charles' plant and g the height of Greg's plant. Both plants are growing exponentially, so we have
$$c = 2 \cdot (1 + 20\%)^t = 2 \cdot (1.2)^t$$
$$\text{and } g = 0.75 \cdot (1 + 60\%)^t = 0.75 \cdot (1.6)^t$$

where t is the number of weeks. We want $g > c$ so
$$0.75 \cdot (1.6)^t > 2 \cdot (1.2)^t.$$

Collecting like terms and simplifying we have
$$\left(\frac{4}{3}\right)^t > \frac{8}{3}.$$

2.6 ZIML March 2019 Division H

Calculating the first few values we have

t	$(4/3)^t$	8/3
1	4/3	8/3
2	16/9	24/9
3	64/27	72/27
4	256/81	216/81

Thus we see week 4 is the first week where Greg's plant is taller and $N = 4$.

Answer: 4

Problem 11 Solution

Using the formula for the transformation, we have

$$A' = (-2 \cdot 2, -2 \cdot 2) = (-4, -4)$$
$$B' = (-2 \cdot 0, -2 \cdot -2) = (0, 4)$$
$$C' = (-2 \cdot 2, -2 \cdot -5) = (-4, 10)$$

giving $\triangle A'B'C'$ as in the diagram below.

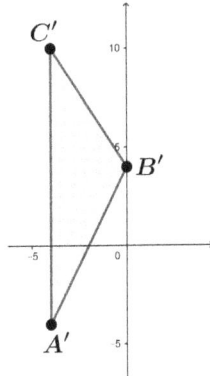

Using $A'C'$ as the base, this is a triangle with base $10 - (-4) = 14$ and height $0 - (-4) = 4$, hence area $\frac{1}{2} \cdot 14 \cdot 4 = 28$.

Note the transformation is a composition of a rotation, reflection, and dilation with a scale factor of 2. Therefore the answer of 28 can also be derived by multiplying the area of $\triangle ABC$ (which is 7) by $2^2 = 4$.

Answer: 28

Problem 12 Solution
$44 = 4 \cdot 11$ so we need the number to be divisible by 4 and by 11.

To be divisible by 4, the last two digits $\overline{B4}$ must be divisible by 4. Therefore
$$B = 0, 2, 4, 6, \text{ or } 8.$$
To be divisible by 11, the alternating sum of the digits must be divisible by 11. Hence
$$4 - B + 9 - 1 + A - 3 = 9 + A - B$$
is divisible by 11. It is impossible for $9 + A - B$ to be 22. Since we want the largest number, we want to maximize A. If $9 + A - B = 11$ then $A - B = 2$. We know B is even so the largest number occurs when $A = 8$ and $B = 6$. This gives the number 381964.

Answer: 381964

Problem 13 Solution
The circle has diameter 4 so $\overline{AB}$ is a diameter. For $\overline{CD}$ to intersect this diameter, we must have C and D on opposite sides of this diameter.

Let O be the center of the circle. Examining triangle $\triangle ACO$ we see $AC = OA = OC = 2$ so the triangle is equilateral. Hence $\widehat{AC} = 60°$. Similarly $\triangle BDO$ has sides 2, 2, and $2\sqrt{2}$ so is a 45-45-90 triangle and $\widehat{BD} = 90°$.

2.6 ZIML March 2019 Division H

Therefore chords $\overline{AB}$ and $\overline{CD}$ intersect at an angle of

$$\frac{1}{2}(60° + 90°) = 150° \div 2 = 75°$$

so $\theta = 75$.

Answer: 75

Problem 14 Solution

We have
$$(1+i\sqrt{3})^2 = 1 + 2i\sqrt{3} + 3i^2$$
$$= -2 + 2i\sqrt{3}.$$

Therefore
$$(1+i\sqrt{3})^3 = (-2+2i\sqrt{3})(1+i\sqrt{3})$$
$$= -2 + 2i\sqrt{3} - 2i\sqrt{3} + 6i^2$$
$$= -8$$

This implies that $(1+i\sqrt{3})^3 = -8$, $(1+i\sqrt{3})^6 = (-8)^2 = 64$, up to $(1+i\sqrt{3})^{99} = (-8)^{33}$ are all integers, 33 in total. Further, no other power is an integer, as it can be written as a power of -8 times either $1+i\sqrt{3}$ or $-2+2i\sqrt{3}$.

Therefore, 33 of the first hundred powers of $1+i\sqrt{3}$ are integers.

Answer: 33

Problem 15 Solution

Calculating prime factorizations we have

$$45 = 3^2 \cdot 5 \text{ and } 200 = 2^3 \cdot 5^2.$$

Therefore M is a multiple of $\text{lcm}(45, 200) = 2^3 \cdot 3^2 \cdot 5^2$.

We want M to have 45 factors. The only way to write 45 as the product of 3 or more non-trivial factors is $45 = 5 \cdot 3 \cdot 3$. Thus we

see the prime factorization of M must be of the form $p^4q^2r^2$ for primes p, q, and r. Therefore we must have $p = 2$, $q = 3$, and $r = 5$ so
$$M = 2^4 \cdot 3^2 \cdot 5^2 = 400 \cdot 9 = 3600,$$
which is our answer.

Answer: 3600

Problem 16 Solution
Expanding $(ax^2 + 3x + 2)^2$ we have
$$a^2x^4 + 9x^2 + 4 + 6ax^3 + 4ax^2 + 12x,$$
so combining like terms we get that
$$f(x) = (4 - a^2)x^4 - 6ax^3 - (4a + 9)x^2 - 12x - 4.$$
For this to be degree 3 we need $4 - a^2 = 0$ so $a = \pm 2$ and since $a > 0$, $a = 2$. Therefore
$$f(x) = -12x^3 - 17x^2 - 12x - 4$$
with leading coefficient -12.

Note by looking at the coefficients individually it is possible to answer the question without completely expanding $f(x)$ as we did above.

Answer: -12

Problem 17 Solution
The ball or sphere has volume $\dfrac{32\pi}{3}$ so using the volume formula $\dfrac{4\pi}{3}r^3$ we see the sphere has radius 2 inches. As the diameter is thus 4 inches this confirms the ball fits nicely in the box. Consider the side view, as shown below, where r denotes the radius of the circle remaining on the top of the sphere.

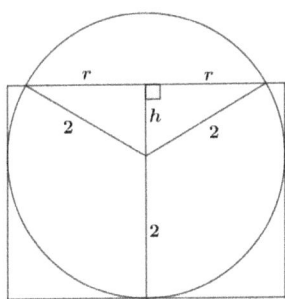

Since the box has a height of 3, $h+2=3$ so $h=1$. Thus using the Pythagorean theorem we have

$$r^2 + h^2 = 2^2 \Rightarrow r^2 + 1 = 4$$

and hence $r = \sqrt{3}$. Therefore the circle's area is $\pi(\sqrt{3})^2 = 3\pi$ and $M = 3$.

Answer: 3

Problem 18 Solution

The die has 6 sides, so there are 6^5 total outcomes.

To get 2 red and thus 3 blue rolls, we first choose which two rolls are red (and the others are blue). This can be done in $\binom{5}{2}$. For each of the red rolls we have 2 choices for which side of the die (1 or 6). Similarly there are 4 choices for each blue roll. Therefore the probability is

$$\frac{\binom{5}{2} \cdot 2^2 \cdot 4^3}{6^5} = \frac{10 \cdot 2^3}{3^5} = \frac{80}{243}.$$

Dividing we have $80 \div 243 \approx 0.329 = 32.9\%$ so rounded to the nearest integer, $K = 33$.

Alternatively we can also calculate the probability using independence:

$$\binom{5}{2}\left(\frac{1}{3}\right)^2\left(\frac{2}{3}\right)^3$$

which leads to the same answer.

Answer: 33

Problem 19 Solution
Shifting the parabolas left 2 units and up 1 unit we'd have parabolas with vertex $(0,0)$ that intersect at $(1,1)$. Hence these shifted parabolas would have equations $y = x^2$ and $x = y^2$ respectively. This means that Parabola 1 has equation

$$y+1 = (x-2)^2$$

and Parabola 2 has equation

$$x-2 = (y+1)^2.$$

The y-intercept of Parabola 1 satisfies $y = (-2)^2 - 1 = 3$ so is $(0,3)$. We are given that the x-intercept of Parabola 2 is $(3,0)$. Therefore the distance between the intercepts is

$$\sqrt{(0-3)^2 + (3-0)^2} = \sqrt{18}$$

with $S = 18$.

Answer: 18

Problem 20 Solution
Counting the number of x-intercepts is the same as counting solutions when $y = 0$, so we use the discriminant.

Calculating the discriminant for the first quadratic we have

$$\Delta = (k-2)^2 - 4(1-k) = k^2.$$

2.6 ZIML March 2019 Division H

Therefore this always has 2 solutions, except when $k = 0$ (when it has 1 solution).

Calculating the discriminant for the second quadratic we have

$$\Delta = (-8)^2 - 4(k^2) = 64 - 4k^2.$$

Hence when $k = 0$ the second quadratic has 2 solutions.

Therefore we must count $k \neq 0$ with $64 - 4k^2 > 0$ (so that both quadratics will have 2 solutions).

$$64 - 4k^2 > 0 \Rightarrow 16 > k^2$$

and hence $-4 < k < 4$. Excluding $k = 0$, there are thus 6 integers k that work.

Answer: 6

2.7 ZIML April 2019 Division H

Below are the solutions from the Division H ZIML Competition held in April 2019.
The problems from the contest are available on p.63.

Problem 1 Solution

Recall any tangent line is perpendicular to the radius of a circle. Further, if two circles are tangent the line segment connecting the two centers contains the tangent point. Therefore A, B, and the two centers form the rectangle shown below:

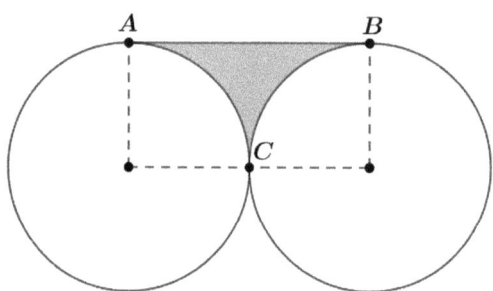

We want to find the perimeter of the shaded region. Each circle has a radius of 2, so $AB = 2 + 2 = 4$. Arcs $\widehat{AC}$ and $\widehat{BC}$ both measure $90°$, so their total arc length is

$$2 \cdot \frac{90°}{360°} \cdot 2\pi \cdot 2 = 2\pi.$$

Using $\pi \approx 3.14$ the perimeter is thus

$$2 \cdot 3.14 + 4 = 6.28 + 4 = 10.28$$

so rounded to the nearest tenth is 10.3.

Answer: 10.3

2.7 ZIML April 2019 Division H

Problem 2 Solution
Using binomial expansion we have
$$(a+b)^4 = a^4 + 4a^3b + 6a^2b^2 + 4ab^3 + b^4.$$

Thus, expanding we have
$$(x+2)^4 = x^4 + 4x^3 \cdot 2 + 6x^2 \cdot 2^2 + 4x \cdot 2^3 + 2^4$$
$$= x^4 + 8x^3 + 24x^2 + 32x + 16$$
and $(x-2)^4 = x^4 + 4x^3 \cdot -2 + 6x^2 \cdot (-2)^2 + 4x \cdot (-2)^3 + (-2)^4$
$$= x^4 - 8x^3 + 24x^2 - 32x + 16.$$

Note the degree 4, degree 2, and constant terms all match. Therefore
$$(x+2)^4 = (x-2)^4$$
$$8x^3 + 32x = -8x^3 - 32x$$
$$16x^3 + 64x = 0$$
$$16x(x^2 + 4) = 0.$$

Hence either $x = 0$ or $x^2 = -4$ so $x = \pm 2i$. Thus $2i = 0 + 2i$ is the one complex root and $A + B = 0 + 2 = 2$.

Answer: 2

Problem 3 Solution
We try to find a pattern in the remainders for both 4^{2019} and 6^{2019}.

For 4^{2019} note $4^2 = 16$ has remainder 7 when divided by 9 and then $4^3 = 64$ has remainder 1 when divided by 9. This pattern continues,
$$4, 7, 1, 4, 7, 1, \ldots.$$
Since 2019 is divisible by 3, 4^{2019} has the same remainder as 4^3 which is 1 when divided by 9.

For 6^{2019} note that $6^2 = 36$ is divisible by 9. Hence any higher power of 6 is also divisible by 9, so 6^{2019} has remainder 0 when divided by 2019.

Therefore $4^{2019} + 6^{2019}$ has remainder $1 + 0 = 1$ when divided by 9.

Answer: 1

Problem 4 Solution

Label the angles in the pentagon a, b, c, d, and e. Focusing on the pentagons near the center we have

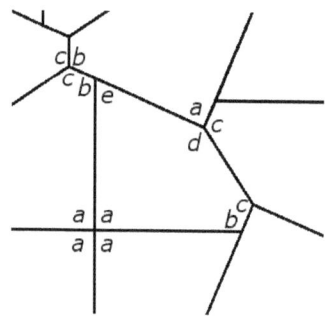

d is the largest angle, so $d = 150°$. Notice $4a = 360°$ so $a = 90°$. Similarly
$$a + d + c = 360°$$
$$90° + 150° + c = 360°$$
$$c = 120°.$$

To find b note
$$b + c + c = 360°$$
$$b + 120° + 120° = 360°$$
$$b = 120°.$$

Finally $b + e = 180°$ so $e = 180° - 120° = 60°$. This is the

2.7 ZIML April 2019 Division H

smallest angle, so 60 is the answer.

Answer: 60

Problem 5 Solution

The minimum value of any parabola with $a > 0$ is at its vertex. We know points with $y = 1$ and $y = 5$ are on our parabola, so the minimum must be ≥ 1.

If the minimum is exactly 1, the vertex must be at the point $(-1, 1)$. Hence the parabola has form

$$y = a(x+1)^2 + 1.$$

Plugging in the point $(3, 5)$ we have

$$a(3+1)^2 + 1 = 5$$
$$16a = 4$$
$$a = \frac{1}{4}$$

Hence $P + Q = 1 + 4 = 5$.

Answer: 5

Problem 6 Solution

There are $5 + 3 = 8$ members of the science club, so 8! different photographs with no restrictions. To count the number of ways at least two of the triplets are together, we subtract off the number of photos with them all apart.

There are 5! ways to arrange the other members of the club. This creates 6 spaces to put the triplets to ensure they are separated. Hence there are $6 \cdot 5 \cdot 4$ ways to position the triplets.

Hence there are
$$8! - 5! \cdot 6 \cdot 5 \cdot 4$$
$$= 6!(8 \cdot 7 - 5 \cdot 4)$$
$$= 720 \cdot 36$$
$$= 25920$$
total photos with at least two of the triplets together.

Answer: 25920

Problem 7 Solution

Factoring $2x^2 - x - 3$ we have $(2x-3)(x+1)$ and $3x+3 = 3(x+1)$ so canceling we can rewrite

$$f(x) = \frac{1}{(2x-3)^2} - \frac{3}{(2x-3)}.$$

To solve $f(x) = 4$ we can clear denominators by multiplying by $(2x-3)^2$. This gives

$$4(2x-3)^2 = 1 - 3(2x-3)$$
$$16x^2 - 48x + 36 = 1 - 6x + 9$$
$$16x^2 - 42x + 26 = 0$$
$$8x^2 - 21x + 13 = 0$$
$$(x-1)(8x-13) = 0$$

Therefore $x = 1$ or $x = \frac{13}{8}$. Since $x > \frac{3}{2}$, the one solution is $x = \frac{13}{8}$ with $P + Q = 13 + 8 = 21$.

Answer: 21

Problem 8 Solution

Consider first only θ in the first quadrant, so $0 \leq \theta < 90°$. Then

$$\sin(\theta) = \cos(\theta) \Rightarrow \frac{\sin(\theta)}{\cos(\theta)} = \tan(\theta) = 1.$$

2.7 ZIML April 2019 Division H

Hence $\theta = 45°$. This implies that $|\sin(\theta)| = |\cos(\theta)|$ for $\theta = 45°, 135°, 225°, 315°, \ldots$. Comparing signs of $\sin(\theta)$ and $\cos(\theta)$ in the four quadrants we have

	I	II	III	IV
$\sin(\theta)$	+	+	−	−
$\cos(\theta)$	+	−	−	+

Thus, in quadrant I, $\theta = 45°$ is a solution to both $|\sin(\theta)| = \cos(\theta)$ and $\sin(\theta) = \cos(\theta)$, while in quadrant IV, $\theta = 315°$ is only a solution to $|\sin(\theta)| = \cos(\theta)$. This is the first such solution, so the answer is 315.

Answer: 315

Problem 9 Solution

Folded up, the net creates the pyramid below, with height h and slant height s.

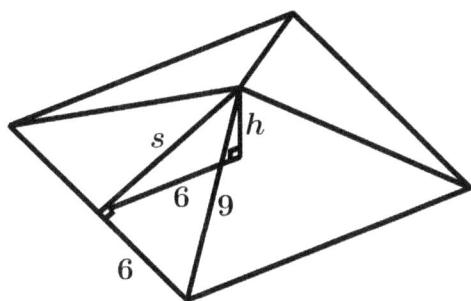

Consider first the lateral face of the pyramid. This is an isosceles triangle with sides 9, 9, and 12, so drawing the altitude (the slant height), gives a right triangle with sides 6, s, and 9. Hence
$$6^2 + s^2 = 9^2$$
$$36 + s^2 = 81$$
$$s^2 = 45$$
$$s = \sqrt{45}$$

The apex of the pyramid is directly above the center of the square base, so the height is part of a triangle with legs 6 and h with hypotenuse $\sqrt{45}$. Thus

$$6^2 + h^2 = (\sqrt{45})^2$$
$$36 + h^2 = 45$$
$$h^2 = 9$$
$$h = 3.$$

Using the volume formula for a pyramid we have $\frac{1}{3} \cdot 12^2 \cdot 3 = 144$ as the answer.

Answer: 144

Problem 10 Solution

Since N contains no perfect squares as factors, N must be the product of primes $p \cdot q \cdot r \cdots$ (all with exponent 1).

For N to be a multiple of 10, $C = 0$ and both 2 and 5 must be factors. In property (iii), $A + C - B = A - B = 0$, so N is a multiple of 11. Hence $2 \cdot 5 \cdot 11 = 110$ is the smallest number that works.

Multiplying by an additional prime will also work, giving

$$2 \cdot 5 \cdot 11 \cdot 3 = 330$$
$$\text{and } 2 \cdot 5 \cdot 11 \cdot 7 = 770$$

as answers as well. ($2 \cdot 5 \cdot 11 \cdot 13$ has 4 digits.) Hence the answer is $110 + 330 + 770 = 1210$.

Answer: 1210

Problem 11 Solution

Consider one of the trapezoids, labeled $ABCD$, with the sides extended to meet the center of the fire pit, O, as shown below.

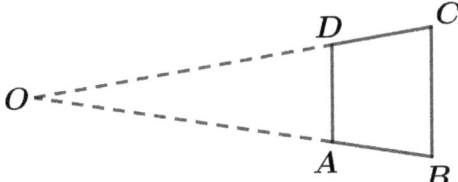

The largest interior angle of $ABCD$ is $99°$, so $\angle A = \angle D = 99°$ (the trapezoid is isosceles). This implies

$$\angle B = \angle C = \angle OAD = \angle ODA = 180° - 99° = 81°.$$

Therefore

$$\angle O = 180° - \angle OAD - \angle ODA = 180° - 2 \cdot 81° = 18°.$$

Note this diagram holds for all of the blocks of the fire pit, so Manny's dad needs $360° \div 18° = 20$ blocks in total.

Answer: 20

Problem 12 Solution

First note $3 \cdot 2^{x+2} = 3 \cdot 2^2 \cdot 2^x = 12 \cdot 2^x$. Similarly $3^{x-1} = \dfrac{1}{3} \cdot 3^x$. Hence after cross multiplying we have

$$4 \cdot 2^x \cdot 3^x = 4 \cdot 6^x = 864.$$

$864 \div 4 = 216 = 6^3$, so $x = 3$. This is the only solution, so our answer is 3.

Answer: 3

Problem 13 Solution

First note all the integers ending in 0 work. This gives 9 numbers (10, 20, up to 90).

The only integers with repeated digits that work are 11, 22, and 33 (with products 1, 4, and 9).

For integers with two different digits, the smaller of these digits is either 1 or 2 (as $3 \cdot 4 = 12$ is too large). If the smaller digit is 1, the second digit can be any of 2 through 9 for 8 possibilities. If the smaller digit is 2, the second digit can be either 3 or 4 for 2 possibilities. Since these two digits can be arranged in either order, there are $2 \cdot (8+2) = 20$ total integers in this case.

Hence there are $9 + 3 + 20 = 32$ two-digit integers who have a product of digits that is a one-digit integer.

Answer: 32

Problem 14 Solution
Using the change of base formula

$$\log_B(A) = \frac{\log_A(A)}{\log_A(B)} = \frac{1}{\log_A(B)}.$$

Hence rewriting the equation gives

$$(\log_A(B))^2 = 4 \rightarrow \log_A(B) = \pm 2.$$

Thus
$$\log_A(B) = 2$$
$$\text{so } A^2 = B$$
$$\text{or } \log_A(B) = -2$$
$$\text{so } A^{-2} = B$$

However, as A and B are both positive integers ≥ 2, the second case is impossible. Hence $A \cdot B = A \cdot A^2 = A^3$. The smallest such value that is at least 100 is $5^3 = 125$.

Answer: 125

2.7 ZIML April 2019 Division H

Problem 15 Solution

The wheel has a circumference of 44 inches, so in moving 110 inches forward, it completes

$$110 \div 44 = \frac{5}{2} = 2.5$$

rotations. Therefore, the spot of paint is now on the ground, creating the following diagram

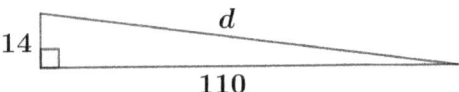

where d is the distance we want. We have

$$d^2 = 14^2 + 110^2 = 196 + 12100 = 12296$$

so $d = \sqrt{12296}$ and $M = 12296$.

Answer: 12296

Problem 16 Solution

Since the ball your friend picked (green because it was winning) was not replaced, box A has 2 green and 2 red balls. Hence you have a $\frac{2}{4} = 50\%$ chance of winning if you get heads and choose a ball from box A.

Box B has 1 green and 4 red balls, so you have a $\frac{1}{5} = 20\%$ chance of winning if you get tails and choose a ball from box B.

Since you have an equal chance of picking from either box (the coin is fair) the probability you win is

$$\frac{1}{2} \cdot 50\% + \frac{1}{2} \cdot 20\% = 35\%$$

so $K = 35$.

Answer: 35

Problem 17 Solution

Let r denote the radius of the base. Using parallel lines r is the adjacent side of a right triangle with an angle of $66.5°$, as shown below.

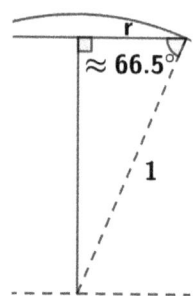

If h is the opposite side of this triangle, then

$$\frac{h}{r} = \tan(66.5°) \approx \frac{23}{10},$$

so $h = \frac{23}{10}r$. Using the Pythagorean theorem we have

$$r^2 + h^2 = 1^2$$
$$r^2 + \left(\frac{23}{10}r\right)^2 = 1$$
$$r^2 + \frac{529}{100}r^2 = 1$$
$$\frac{629}{100}r^2 = 1$$
$$r^2 = \frac{100}{629}$$

Therefore the area of the base is

$$\pi r^2 \approx \frac{22}{7} \cdot \frac{100}{629} = \frac{2200}{4403}$$

with $P+Q = 6603$.

Answer: 6603

Problem 18 Solution

First consider the domain. For both square roots to be defined $x+4 \geq 0$ so $x \geq -4$ and $16-x > 0$ so $x < 16$. So $-4 \leq x < 16$.

For $y < 0$ we need

$$\sqrt{x+4} < \frac{8}{\sqrt{16-x}}$$

$$x+4 < \frac{64}{16-x}$$

$$(4+x)(16-x) < 64$$

$$64 + 12x - x^2 < 64$$

$$x(12-x) < 0$$

$x(12-x)$ is negative if $x < 0$ or if $x > 12$. Combining this with the domain we have

$$-4 \leq x < 0 \text{ or } 12 < x < 16.$$

Thus there are $4+3 = 7$ integer x with $y < 0$.

Answer: 7

Problem 19 Solution

We are only given a formula for $f(n)$ if n is a power of a prime. Hence first write $9000 = 3^2 \cdot 1000$ so

$$f(9000) = f(3^2) \cdot f(1000) = 3 \cdot f(1000)$$

because $f(3^2) = 2+1 = 3$. For $f(1000)$ we similarly have, using $1000 = 2^3 \cdot 5^3$,

$$f(1000) = f(2^3) \cdot f(5^3) = 4 \cdot 4 = 16.$$

Combining we have $f(9000) = 3 \cdot 16 = 48$.

Note, in general, $f(n)$ gives a formula for the number of factors of n.

Answer: 48

Problem 20 Solution
Consider the diagram below

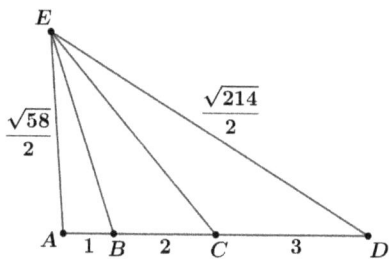

Since we know the three sides of $\triangle ADE$, we can use the Law of Cosines to find $\cos \angle EAD$ and then use this to find BE and CE. We have

$$DE^2 = AE^2 + AD^2 - 2 \cdot AE \cdot AD \cdot \cos \angle EAD$$
$$\frac{214}{4} = \frac{58}{4} + 36 - 2 \cdot \frac{\sqrt{58}}{2} \cdot 6 \cdot \cos \angle EAD$$
$$3 = -6\sqrt{58} \cos \angle EAD$$

so $\cos \angle EAD = \dfrac{1}{-2\sqrt{58}}$. (We leave this unsimplified because it will cancel nicely.) Thus

$$BE^2 = AE^2 + AB^2 - 2 \cdot AE \cdot AB \cdot \cos \angle EAD$$
$$BE^2 = \frac{58}{4} + 1 - 2 \cdot \frac{\sqrt{58}}{2} \cdot 1 \cdot \frac{1}{-2\sqrt{58}}$$
$$BE^2 = \frac{29}{2} + 1 + \frac{1}{2}$$
$$BE^2 = 16$$

so $BE = 4$. Similarly

$$CE^2 = AE^2 + AC^2 - 2 \cdot AE \cdot AC \cdot \cos \angle EAD$$
$$CE^2 = \frac{58}{4} + 9 - 2 \cdot \frac{\sqrt{58}}{2} \cdot 3 \cdot \frac{1}{-2\sqrt{58}}$$
$$CE^2 = \frac{29}{2} + 9 + \frac{3}{2}$$
$$CE^2 = 25$$

so $CE = 5$. Therefore the perimeter of $\triangle BCE = 2 + 5 + 4 = 11$.

Answer: 11

2.8 ZIML May 2019 Division H

Below are the solutions from the Division H ZIML Competition held in May 2019.
The problems from the contest are available on p.73.

Problem 1 Solution
Rhombus $CDGH$ has perimeter, so each of its sides have length $8 \div 4 = 2$. Therefore
$$AB = CD = EF = CH = GD = GH = 2.$$
As $AG : GD = 3 : 1$, $AG = 3 \cdot 2 = 6$. Similarly $FG = 2 \cdot 2 = 4$. Thus
$$BC = BH + CH = 6 + 2 = 8$$
$$\text{and } CE = CD + DE = 2 + 4 = 6.$$
Hence the entire figure has
$$AB + BC + CE + EF + FG + GA$$
$$= 2 + 8 + 6 + 2 + 4 + 6$$
$$= 28$$
as its perimeter.

Answer: 28

Problem 2 Solution
There are two parts to Greg's claim. First, he claims "All mice with the gene have black eyes." The 35 mice that have the gene and black eyes support this half of the claim.

Second, he claims "No mice without the gene have black eyes." The 70 mice without the gene and pink eyes (not black) support this half of the claim.

Therefore $35 + 70 = 105$ of 150 mice support his claim, which is
$$\frac{105}{150} = \frac{7}{10} = 70\%$$

ZOOM INTERNATIONAL MATH LEAGUE: ziml.areteem.org

of the mice. Hence $K = 70$.

Answer: 70

Problem 3 Solution
Looking at the prime factorizations, 53 is prime, $54 = 2 \cdot 3^3$, and $55 = 5 \cdot 11$. Hence,

$$53 \cdot 54 \cdot 55 = 2 \cdot 3^3 \cdot 5 \cdot 11 \cdot 53,$$

so it has

$$(1+1)(3+1)(1+1)(1+1)(1+1) = 64$$

factors in total.

Answer: 64

Problem 4 Solution
The new solid has $4 + 4 + 1 = 9$ vertices. Therefore any path containing all 9 vertices will need to contain at least $9 - 1 = 8$ edges.

All of the edges of the cube are length 4, while the lateral edges of the pyramid have length 3. Since the lateral in the pyramid are shorter, we want to use as many of those edges as possible. However, we do not want to visit any vertex more than once (else we will need more than 9 edges) so we can use at most 2 of these lateral edges.

Hence we use 2 lateral edges from the pyramid and $8 - 2 = 6$ edges from the cube. Many such paths are then possible, but one example is shown below:

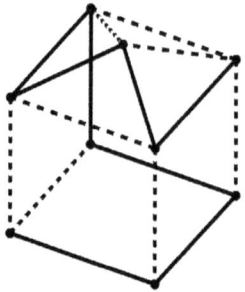

Therefore the shortest path has length $6 \cdot 4 + 2 \cdot 3 = 30$.

Answer: 30

Problem 5 Solution

We find the last digits of 7^{79} and 9^{79} separately and then add them together.

For 7^{79} the pattern in the last digit is

$$7, 9, 3, 1, \ldots$$

with the pattern repeating every 4 terms. 76 is a multiple of 4, so the last digit of 7^{79} is the third in the pattern, which is 3.

For 9^{79} the pattern in the last digit is

$$9, 1, \ldots$$

with the pattern repeating every 2 terms. 79 is odd, so 9^{79} has last digit 9.

Adding them together $3 + 9 = 12$ so the last digit of $7^{79} + 9^{79}$ is 2.

Answer: 2

2.8 ZIML May 2019 Division H

Problem 6 Solution

We first find the lengths AB, BC, and AC. AB is the hypotenuse of a right triangle with side lengths $6 \div 2 = 3$ (on the top of the cube). Thus

$$AB = \sqrt{3^2 + 3^2} = \sqrt{18} = 3\sqrt{2}.$$

Similarly, $BC = AC$ are the hypotenuses of right triangles with side lengths 3 and 6, so

$$BC = AC = \sqrt{6^2 + 3^2} = \sqrt{45} = 3\sqrt{5}.$$

Therefore $\triangle ABC$ is isosceles, so it can be split into two right triangles as in the diagram below.

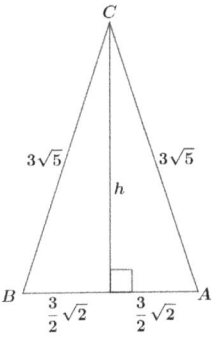

Using the Pythagorean theorem,

$$\left(\frac{3}{2}\sqrt{2}\right)^2 + h^2 = (3\sqrt{5})^2$$

$$\frac{9}{2} + h^2 = 45$$

$$h^2 = \frac{81}{2}$$

$$h = \frac{9}{\sqrt{2}}$$

Hence the area of $\triangle ABC$ is
$$\frac{1}{2} \cdot \frac{3}{2}\sqrt{2} \cdot \frac{9}{\sqrt{2}} = \frac{27}{2}.$$
Thus, the answer (as a decimal) is 13.5.

Answer: 13.5

Problem 7 Solution

If $x = 2$ is a solution, then
$$|2-6| = 2\sqrt{2+K}$$
$$4 = 2\sqrt{2+K}$$
$$2 = \sqrt{2+K}$$
$$4 = 2+K$$
$$2 = K$$

Therefore we must solve $|x-6| = 2\sqrt{x+2}$. Squaring both sides and factoring gives
$$(x-6)^2 = 4(x+2)$$
$$x^2 - 12x + 36 = 4x + 8$$
$$x^2 - 16x + 28 = 0$$
$$(x-2)(x-14) = 0$$

so $x = 2$ and $x = 14$ are solutions. Thus the other solution is 14.

Answer: 14

Problem 8 Solution

First calculate $\widehat{DB}$.
$$\frac{1}{2}(\widehat{DB} - \widehat{BC}) = 25°$$
$$\widehat{DB} - 55° = 50°$$
$$\widehat{DB} = 105°$$

2.8 ZIML May 2019 Division H

Therefore, major arc $\widehat{CD}$ measures

$$360° - 55° - 105° = 200°.$$

If r is the radius of the circle, then (using the arc length of $\widehat{CD}$)

$$\frac{200°}{360°} \cdot 2\pi r = 30\pi$$

$$\frac{10}{9}\pi r = 30\pi$$

$$r = 27.$$

Thus the circle has area $\pi \cdot 27^2 = 729\pi$ so $K = 729$.

Answer: 729

Problem 9 Solution

When $M = 0$, the graphs $y = |5x|$ and $y = -1$ do not intersect.

The graph of $y = |5x|$ is symmetric with respect to the y-axis with $y \geq 0$ for all x. Therefore if the graphs of $y = |5x|$ and $y = Mx - 1$ intersect for a value of $M = k > 0$, they will also intersect when $M = -k < 0$. We focus on the case when $M > 0$.

If $M > 0$, the graphs must intersect when $x > 0$ (as $y = Mx - 1$ has positive slope). When $x > 0$, $y = |5x| = 5x$ so we just need $y = 5x$ and $y = Mx - 1$ to intersect with $x > 0$. This will only happen if $M > 5$ (when $y = Mx - 1$ has a larger slope). Therefore the graphs do not intersect when $M = 1, 2, \ldots, 5$.

Thus, $y = |5x|$ and $y = Mx - 1$ do not intersect if

$$M = -5, -4, \ldots, 5,$$

11 in total.

Answer: 11

Problem 10 Solution

First note

$$D(T) = 10{,}000 \cdot \left(\frac{64}{729}\right)^{T+2}$$

$$= 10{,}000 \cdot \left(\frac{64}{729}\right)^2 \cdot \left(\frac{64}{729}\right)^T.$$

Thus to find $\dfrac{B}{C}$ we need to focus in $\left(\dfrac{64}{729}\right)^T$.

T represents quarters, which consist of 3 months, so $3T = t$ or $T = \dfrac{t}{T}$ where t is measured in months. Hence

$$\left(\frac{64}{729}\right)^T = \left(\frac{64}{729}\right)^{t/3}$$

$$= \left(\frac{64^{1/3}}{729^{1/3}}\right)^t$$

$$= \left(\frac{4}{9}\right)^t$$

and $B + C = 4 + 9 = 13$.

Answer: 13

Problem 11 Solution

For any circle and tangent line, the radius of the circle to the tangent point is perpendicular to the tangent line. Thus the line perpendicular to the line $y = 2x + 3$ must contain the center of the circle $(0,0)$.

The line $y = 2x + 3$ has slope 2, so we want the line with slope $-\dfrac{1}{2}$ containing $(0,0)$, which is $y = -\dfrac{1}{2}x$. This intersects the line

2.8 ZIML May 2019 Division H

$y = 2x+3$ when
$$2x+3 = -\frac{1}{2}x$$
$$\frac{5}{2}x = -3$$
$$x = -\frac{6}{5}$$

This implies
$$y = -\frac{1}{2} \cdot -\frac{6}{5} = \frac{3}{5}.$$

Using the distance formula, the radius of the circle is

$$R = \sqrt{\left(-\frac{6}{5}\right)^2 + \left(\frac{3}{5}\right)^2}$$
$$= \sqrt{\frac{36}{25} + \frac{9}{25}}$$
$$= \sqrt{\frac{45}{25}}$$
$$= \sqrt{\frac{9}{5}}$$

Therefore $M = R^2 = \frac{9}{5} = 1.8.$

Answer: 1.8

Problem 12 Solution

The number must be a multiple of 4 and 5, so it is a multiple of $4 \cdot 5 = 20$. Hence the last two digits
$$\overline{BC} = 00, 20, 40, 60, \text{ or } 80.$$

To be a multiple of 9, the sum of the digits
$$A + 3 + 4 + B + C = 7 + A + B + C$$

must also be a multiple of 9. We want the largest number, so A needs to be as large as possible. If $A = 9$, then $B+C+16$ must be a multiple of 9, which happens when $\overline{BC} = 20$. Thus the 5-digit number is 93420.

Answer: 93420

Problem 13 Solution

Because the numbers increase left to right and top to bottom, the number 1 (the smallest) must be in the top-left corner and similarly 6 (the largest) must be in the lower-left corner.

The next smallest number 2 must be as far left as possible in either the first or second row, giving two possibilities:

1	2	
		6

or

1		
2		6

Identical reasoning for 3 leads to the three possibilities below:

1	2	3
		6

or

1	2	
3		6

or

1	3	
2		6

In the first case, the remaining 4 and 5 must be placed in the bottom row (in that order), so there is only 1 way to finish the table. In both the second and third cases, the 4 and 5 can be arranged in either way, for 2 additional ways for each case.

Therefore there are $1+2+2 = 5$ total ways to fill in the table.

Answer: 5

Problem 14 Solution

The 6 angles in a hexagon add up to $180°(6-2) = 180° \cdot 4 = 720°$. If d is the common difference in the arithmetic sequence, then the 6 angles in the hexagon measure

$$126-4d, 126-3d, 126-2d, 126-d, 126, 126+d$$

in degrees. Adding them up we have

$$6 \cdot 126 - 9d = 720$$
$$756 - 9d = 720$$
$$-9d = -36$$
$$d = 4.$$

Thus the smallest angle is $126 - 4 \cdot 4 = 110$.

Answer: 110

Problem 15 Solution
Doubling the second and third equations gives

$$3x - 2\log_2(y) + 3^z = 5$$
$$4x + 2\log_2(y) - 2 \cdot 3^z = 6$$
$$16x + 2\log_2(y) - 4 \cdot 3^z = 4$$

Then, adding the first equation to the second and third eliminates y, giving

$$7x - 3^z = 11$$
$$19x + -3 \cdot 3^z = 9$$

Multiplying the first equation by -3 gives $21x + 3 \cdot 3^z = -33$. Adding this to the other equation eliminates the variable z:

$$-2x = -24 \Rightarrow x = 12,$$

which gives our answer.

(Note in all the above work, we are solving a standard linear system of equations with variables x, $\log_2(y)$, and 3^z.)

Answer: 12

Problem 16 Solution

The graph of $y = x^2 - mx - 4m$ has no x-intercepts if the discriminant of $x^2 - mx - 4m$ is less than zero. Therefore

$$(-m)^2 - 4 \cdot 1 \cdot (-4m) < 0$$
$$m^2 + 16m < 0$$
$$m(m+16) < 0.$$

For $m(m+16) < 0$ we must have $m < 0$ and $m+16 > 0$ or $m > -16$. Since m is an integer,

$$m = -15, -14, \ldots, -1$$

with sum

$$-15 + -14 + \cdots + -1 = -1 \cdot \frac{15 \cdot 16}{2} = -120$$

using that the sum of the first n integers is $\frac{n(n+1)}{2}$.

Answer: -120

Problem 17 Solution

Since $x = 2 - i\sqrt{3}$ is a solution, so is its complex conjugate $x = 2 + i\sqrt{3}$. Therefore, using the factor theorem,

$$\begin{aligned} x^2 + Bx + C &= (x - (2 - i\sqrt{3}))(x - (2 + i\sqrt{3})) \\ &= x^2 - 4x + 7. \end{aligned}$$

The constant term is the result of the difference of two squares

$$(2 - i\sqrt{3})(2 + i\sqrt{3}) = 4 - 3i^2 = 4 + 3 = 7.$$

Thus, $B = -4$ and $C = 7$, with $B \cdot C = -4 \cdot 7 = -28$.

Answer: -28

2.8 ZIML May 2019 Division H

Problem 18 Solution
There are 30 cards in total. Since Logan picks the cards with replacement and the order does not matter, there are

$$\binom{30}{4} = \frac{30 \cdot 29 \cdot 28 \cdot 27}{4 \cdot 3 \cdot 2 \cdot 1} = 15 \cdot 29 \cdot 7 \cdot 9$$

total outcomes.

Logan wants all the cards to be the same color, so there are 3 choices for the color. The cards should also be in numerical order, so they must be $1,2,3,4$ or $2,3,4,5$ up to $7,8,9,10$. (Recall the order does not matter, so we only worry about which numbers are chosen.) Hence there are 7 choices for the numbers.

This gives a probability of

$$(3 \cdot 7) \div \binom{30}{4} = \frac{3 \cdot 7}{15 \cdot 29 \cdot 7 \cdot 9} = \frac{1}{15 \cdot 29 \cdot 3} = \frac{1}{1305},$$

with $Q - P = 1305 - 1 = 1304$.

Answer: 1304

Problem 19 Solution
Since $8 = 2^3$, if $M = 2 \cdot 8^8$ then $M = 2 \cdot (2^3)^8$ so $M = 2^{25}$. Therefore

$$\log_{1/5}(\log_2 M) = \log_{1/5}(\log_2 2^{25})$$
$$= \log_{1/5} 25$$
$$= -2,$$

as $\left(\frac{1}{5}\right)^{-2} = 25.$

Hence we want N such that $\log_{1/2}(\log_5 N) = -2$. Thus

$$\log_5 N = \left(\frac{1}{2}\right)^{-2}$$
$$\log_5 N = 4$$
$$N = 5^4$$

so $N = 625$.

Answer: 625

Problem 20 Solution

Let $AE = CD = x$ and $AD = y$. We want to solve for x. Using $\cos(\angle A) = \dfrac{\sqrt{5}}{3}$ we have (in $\triangle ADE$),

$$\frac{AD}{AE} = \frac{y}{x} = \frac{\sqrt{5}}{3} \Rightarrow y = \frac{\sqrt{5}}{3}x.$$

Note

$$\sin^2(\angle A) = 1 - \cos^2(\angle A) = 1 - \frac{5}{9} = \frac{4}{9}$$

so $\sin(\angle A) = \dfrac{2}{3}$. Hence (in $\triangle ABC$)

$$\frac{BC}{AC} = \frac{8}{x+y} = \frac{2}{3} \Rightarrow x+y = 12.$$

Substituting gives

$$x + \frac{\sqrt{5}}{3}x = 12$$
$$3x + \sqrt{5}x = 36$$
$$x(3 + \sqrt{5}) = 36$$
$$x = \frac{36}{3+\sqrt{5}}.$$

Finally, multiplying by $3-\sqrt{5}$ in the numerator and denominator

$$x = \frac{36(3-\sqrt{5})}{9-5} = 9(3-\sqrt{5}) = 27 - 9\sqrt{5}.$$

Hence $S + T = 27 + -9 = 18$.

Answer: 18

2.9 ZIML June 2019 Division H

Below are the solutions from the Division H ZIML Competition held in June 2019.
The problems from the contest are available on p.81.

Problem 1 Solution
The internal angles of a regular pentagon are

$$\frac{180°(5-2)}{5} = 36° \cdot 3 = 108°.$$

Similarly the internal angles of a regular hexagon are

$$\frac{180°(6-2)}{6} = 30° \cdot 4 = 120°.$$

Since the pentagon has a side length of 6 the right triangle has a hypotenuse of 6. One of the legs is $2\sqrt{3}$ (the side of the hexagon). Recognizing $2\sqrt{3} \cdot \sqrt{3} = 6$, this triangle is a 30-60-90 triangle. Therefore in this triangle $\angle A = 30°$. This implies that

$$\angle BAC = 360° - 108° - 120° - 30°$$
$$= 102°$$

which is our answer.

Answer: 102

Problem 2 Solution
There are 4 vowels (U, E, I, E) and 6 consonants (S, M, M, R, T, M) in SUMMERTIME. Once the vowels are placed, there is one way to arrange them (in the order E, E, I, U), so there are

$$\binom{10}{6} = \frac{10 \cdot 9 \cdot 8 \cdot 7}{4 \cdot 3 \cdot 2 \cdot 1} = 210$$

was to choose (and arrange) where the vowels are placed in the rearrangement of the 10 letters.

The remaining 6 letters can be arranged in 6! ways, however, we need to divide by 3! to account for the three repeated M's. Hence there are
$$\frac{6!}{3!} = 5! = 120$$
ways to arrange the consonants.

Combining we have
$$210 \cdot 120 = 25200$$
arrangements in total.

Answer: 25200

Problem 3 Solution

If $x = -2$ is a root, then $x+2$ is a factor. Similarly, roots of $\frac{2}{3}$, $2i$, and $-2i$ imply that
$$(3x-2), (x-2i), \text{ and } (x+2i)$$
are factors of $P(x)$. Hence $P(x)$ is a multiple of
$$(x+2)(3x-2)(x-2i)(x+2i)$$
$$= (3x^2 + 4x - 4)(x^2 + 4)$$
$$= 3x^4 + 4x^3 + 8x^2 + 16x - 16.$$

Since $P(x)$ has leading coefficient 12, we must multiply by 4. This gives
$$P(x) = 12x^4 + 16x^3 + 32x^2 + 64x - 64,$$
with $B + C + D + E = 16 + 32 + 64 - 64 = 48$.

Answer: 48

Problem 4 Solution

Since 5 males and 3 females forgot their apron, $5+3=8$ students forgot their apron. None of them forgot both their apron and their hat, but everyone forgot something, so there were $20-8=12$ people who forgot their hats, $11-3=8$ of them female. Thus, $12-8=4$ males forgot their hat.

We can summarize this information in the following two-way table.

	Apron	Hat	Total
Male	5	4	9
Female	3	8	11
Total	8	12	20

Hence, the probability that a randomly chosen student who forgot their hat is male is $\frac{4}{12} = \frac{1}{3}$. Therefore $Q - P = 3 - 1 = 2$.

Answer: 2

Problem 5 Solution

Any 30-60-90 triangle has side lengths in ratio $1 : \sqrt{3} : 2$ and any 45-45-90 triangle has side lengths in ratio $1 : 1 : \sqrt{2}$.

Let x denote the length of the hypotenuse of triangle A which is also the length of the leg of triangle B. The hypotenuse of triangle B, which is also the hypotenuse of triangle C, therefore has length
$$x \cdot \sqrt{2} = x\sqrt{2}.$$
Thus the longer leg of triangle C, which is also the leg of triangle D has length
$$x\sqrt{2} \cdot \frac{\sqrt{3}}{2} = \frac{x\sqrt{6}}{2}.$$
Lastly, the hypotenuse of triangle D, which is also the hypotenuse of triangle E has length
$$\frac{x\sqrt{6}}{2} \cdot \sqrt{2} = x\sqrt{3}.$$

2.9 ZIML June 2019 Division H

Therefore triangles A and E are similar, with ratio of sides $x : x\sqrt{3} = 1 : \sqrt{3}$. This means their ratio of areas is $1^2 : \sqrt{3}^2 = 1 : 3$ and thus the area of triangle E is $90 \cdot 3 = 270$.

Answer: 270

Problem 6 Solution
We have that $64 = 2^6$ and $128 = 2^7$ so we can rewrite both sides of the equation as powers of 2. Hence

$$64^{3x+2} = 128^{x-4}$$
$$(2^6)^{3x+2} = (2^7)^{x-4}$$
$$2^{18x+12} = 2^{7x-28}$$
$$18x + 12 = 7x - 28$$
$$11x = -40$$
$$x = \frac{-40}{11}$$

so $Q - P = 11 - (-40) = 51$.

Answer: 51

Problem 7 Solution
$y = -x^2 + Mx - 3$ is a parabola opening downward. If its maximum value is less than M, then the parabola and the line $y = M$ do not intersect. Hence

$$-x^2 + Mx - 3 = M$$
or equivalently $x^2 - Mx + (M+3) = 0$

has no real solutions. Calculating the discriminant we have

$$(-M)^2 - 4 \cdot 1 \cdot (M+3) < 0$$
$$M^2 - 4M - 12 < 0$$
$$(M+2)(M-6) < 0$$

Thus if $-2 < M < 6$ the discriminant is negative (as then $M+2 > 0$ but $M-6 < 0$). This gives the integers

$$M = -1, 0, 1, \ldots, 5$$

a total of 7 integers.

Answer: 7

Problem 8 Solution

The Pythagorean theorem tells us that

$$10^2 + BE^2 = AE^2$$
$$5^2 + EC^2 = EF^2$$
$$AE^2 + EF^2 = AF^2$$

and

$$AD^2 + 5^2 = AF^2.$$

Combining these equations we have

$$(10^2 + BE^2) + (5^2 + EC^2) = (AD^2 + 5^2).$$

Since E is the midpoint of BC and $AD = BC$, we have $BE = EC$ and $AD = 2 \cdot BE$, so we can rewrite the equation as

$$10^2 + 2 \cdot BE^2 = (2 \cdot BE)^2,$$

so $2 \cdot BE^2 = 100$, and $BE = 5\sqrt{2}$. This means $AD = 2 \times 5\sqrt{2} = \sqrt{200}$, so $K = 200$.

Answer: 200

Problem 9 Solution

We look for a pattern in the remainders when powers of 6 are divided by 50:

Number	6^1	6^2	6^3	6^4	6^5	6^6
Remainder	6	36	16	46	26	6

2.9 ZIML June 2019 Division H

Since 6^6 has the same remainder as 6^1 when divided by 50, we see that the pattern repeats every 5 terms. Thus 6^{5050} has the same remainder as 6^5, which is 26.

Answer: 26

Problem 10 Solution

Let $x = m\widehat{DB}$ so $m\widehat{BE} = m\widehat{EC} = 2x$. As $\overline{DC}$ is a diameter,

$$x + 2x + 2x = 180°$$
$$5x = 180°$$
$$x = 36°,$$

Therefore
$$m\widehat{DE} = m\widehat{EA}$$
$$= x + 2x$$
$$= 108°$$

and thus in $\triangle ADE$,

$$\angle A = \angle D = 108° \div 2 = 54°.$$

This implies that
$$\angle E = 180° - 108° = 72°,$$

which is the largest in $\triangle ADE$. Thus 72 is our answer.

Answer: 72

Problem 11 Solution

According to the Rational Root Theorem, $\pm\dfrac{P}{Q}$ are possible roots of a polynomial, if P is a factor of the constant term and Q is a factor of the leading coefficient.

For this problem, the leading term is

$$x \cdot 2x \cdot x \cdot x = 2x^4$$

and hence $Q = 1$ or $Q = 2$. Similarly the constant term is
$$-1 \cdot 1 \cdot -3 \cdot 3 = 9$$
and $P = 1$, $P = 3$, or $P = 9$. Thus,
$$\pm 1, \pm 3, \pm 9, \pm \frac{1}{2}, \pm \frac{3}{2}, \pm \frac{9}{2}$$
are possible roots according to the Rational Root Theorem, a total of 12. As it is clear that
$$x = 1, x = -\frac{1}{2}, x = 3, \text{ and } x = -3$$
are the solutions, we have
$$\frac{4}{12} = \frac{1}{3} = 33.\overline{3}\%$$
of the possible rational roots are actual roots. Thus K rounded to the nearest integer is 33.

Answer: 33

Problem 12 Solution
A cone with height h and radius r has volume
$$\frac{1}{3}\pi r^2 h$$
and a sphere with radius $\frac{r}{3}$ has volume
$$\frac{4}{3}\pi \left(\frac{r}{3}\right)^3 = \frac{4}{81}\pi r^3.$$
Hence if the two have the same volume
$$\frac{1}{3}\pi r^2 h = \frac{4}{81}\pi r^3$$
$$27h = 4r$$
$$\frac{h}{r} = \frac{4}{27}.$$

2.9 ZIML June 2019 Division H

Thus $P+Q = 4+27 = 31$.

Answer: 31

Problem 13 Solution
We use the notation A^c, etc. to denote complement.

A and B are mutually exclusive, so $P(A \cap B) = 0$ (there is no overlap). This also implies that $P(A \cap B \cap C) = 0$. Therefore if $P(A \cap C) = 0.1$, then $P(A \cap C \cap B^c) = 0.1$ and identical reasoning shows $P(B \cap C \cap A^c) = 0.1$. This allows us to calculate all the portions of a Venn diagram for A, B, and C as shown below:

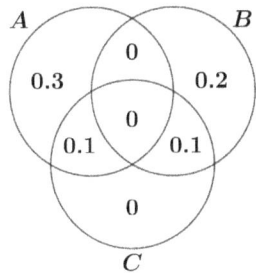

(For example, $P(A \cap B^c \cap C^c) = 0.4 - 0.1 = 0.3$.) Hence

$$P(A \cup B \cup C) = 0.3 + 0.2 + 0.1 + 0.1 = 0.7$$

gives our answer.

Note: It is also possible to calculate the answer using the principle of inclusion-exclusion.

Answer: 0.7

Problem 14 Solution
Since 2 and 5 are both factors of $\overline{abcd}$ and $\overline{abcde}$, both numbers are factors of 10, and hence $d = e = 0$.

3 is a factor of $\overline{ab}$, so $a+b$ is a multiple of 3. Similarly 3 is a factor of $\overline{abc}$, so $a+b+c$ is also a multiple of 3. This implies the difference, digit c, is also a multiple of 3. As 2 is also a factor of $\overline{abc}$, c is either 0 or 6.

2 is a factor of $\overline{a}$ and $\overline{ab}$, so digits a and b are also even. Since $a+b$ must be a multiple of 3, the largest leading digits possible are $a=8$ and $b=4$. For $\overline{abc}$ to be divisible by 4, c must be 0.

Hence the largest number satisfying all the restrictions is 84000.

Answer: 84000

Problem 15 Solution
Since $\sin^2(A) + \cos^2(A) = 1$, we have

$$\cos(A) = \pm\sqrt{1 - \left(\frac{2\sqrt{42}}{17}\right)^2}$$

$$= \pm\sqrt{1 - \frac{168}{289}}$$

$$= \pm\sqrt{\frac{121}{289}}$$

$$= \pm\frac{11}{17}.$$

Since we know $\triangle ABC$ is acute, we must have that $\cos(A) = \frac{11}{17}$.

Thus using the law of cosines we have

$$BC^2 = AB^2 + AC^2 - 2 \cdot AB \cdot AC \cdot \cos(A)$$

$$= 12^2 + 17^2 - 2 \cdot 12 \cdot 17 \cdot \frac{11}{17}$$

$$= 433 - 264$$

$$= 169.$$

2.9 ZIML June 2019 Division H

Therefore $BC = \sqrt{169} = 13$.

Answer: 13

Problem 16 Solution
The two points $(2,5)$ and $(6,5)$ have the same y-value. This implies that the axis of symmetry of the parabola is $x = (2+6) \div 2 = 4$, so the parabola can be written in the form
$$y - k = a(x-4)^2.$$
The y-value of the vertex is k. Plugging in the point $(6,5)$ gives
$$5 - k = a(6-4)^2 \Rightarrow 5 - k = 4a.$$
Similarly, using the point $(7,6)$,
$$6 - k = a(7-4)^2 \Rightarrow 6 - k = 9a.$$
Subtracting we have $1 = 5a$ so $a = \dfrac{1}{5}$. Substituting back in,
$$5 - k = 4 \cdot \frac{1}{5} \Rightarrow k = 5 - \frac{4}{5}.$$
Therefore, $k = 4.2$ when expressed as a decimal.

Answer: 4.2

Problem 17 Solution
The distance from A to $\overline{BC}$ is the length of the perpendicular line segment $\overline{BD}$ as shown in the diagram below.

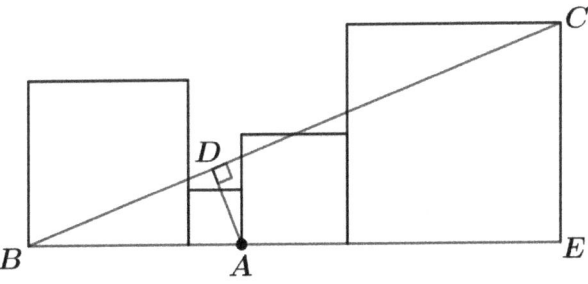

Triangles $\triangle BAD$ and $\triangle BCE$ are right triangles that share $\angle B$, so $\triangle BAD \sim \triangle BCE$. We have

$$BA = 3+1 = 4 \text{ and } BE = 1+2+3+4 = 10$$

with

$$BC = \sqrt{BE^2 + CE^2} = \sqrt{10^2 + 4^2} = \sqrt{116}.$$

Using the similar triangles:

$$BC/CE = BA/AD$$
$$AD \cdot BC = BA \cdot CE$$
$$AD \cdot \sqrt{116} = 4 \cdot 4$$

Simplifying we have

$$AD = \frac{16}{\sqrt{116}}$$
$$= \frac{8}{\sqrt{29}}$$
$$= \frac{8\sqrt{29}}{29}.$$

Therefore $R + S + T = 8 + 29 + 29 = 66$.

Answer: 66

Problem 18 Solution
Let $a + bi = x$. Then

$$(4-i) + x = (4-i) \cdot x.$$

Even though this equation has imaginary numbers, it is still a linear equation. Solving for x we have

$$(4-i)x - x = (4-i)$$
$$(3-i)x = (4-i)$$
$$x = \frac{4-i}{3-i}$$

2.9 ZIML June 2019 Division H

Simplifying,
$$x = \frac{4-i}{3-i} \cdot \frac{3+i}{3+i} = \frac{13+i}{10}$$
so $a = \frac{13}{10}$ and $b = \frac{1}{10}$. Therefore
$$a^2 + b^2 = \left(\frac{13}{10}\right)^2 + \left(\frac{1}{10}\right)^2$$
$$= \frac{169}{100} + \frac{1}{100}$$
$$= \frac{170}{100}.$$
Written as a decimal, $a^2 + b^2 = 1.7$.

Answer: 1.7

Problem 19 Solution
The line $y = 0.5x + 2$ intersects the x-axis when $0.5x + 2 = 0$ or $x = -4$. When $x = 3$,
$$y = 0.5 \cdot 3 + 2 = 3.5.$$
Similarly, the line $y = 5 - x$ intersects the x-axis when $x = 5$ and when $x = 3$,
$$y = 5 - 3 = 2.$$
Therefore the area below this graph and above the x-axis (shown below), can be split up into two triangles.

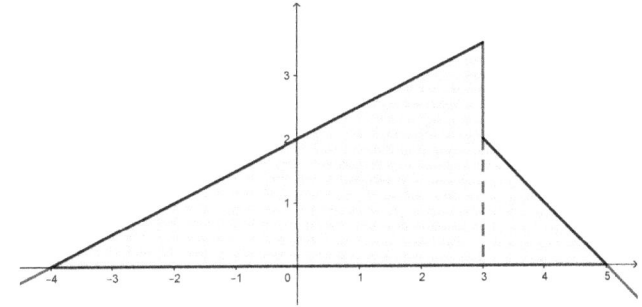

The larger triangle has a base of $3-(-4)=7$ and a height of 3.5 so area
$$\frac{1}{2} \cdot 7 \cdot 3.5 = 12.25.$$
The other triangle has a base of $5-3=2$ and a height of 2, so area
$$\frac{1}{2} \cdot 2 \cdot 2 = 2.$$
Hence the combined area is $12.25 + 2 = 14.25$.

Answer: 14.25

Problem 20 Solution
The prime factorization of $144 = 12^2$ is $2^4 \cdot 3^2$. Therefore
$$f(144) = 4^2 \cdot 2^3 = 2^4 \cdot 2^3 = 2^7.$$
Thus $f(144)$ has $7+1=8$ factors.

Answer: 8

3. Appendix

3.1 Division H Topics Covered

Algebra

- Students should be comfortable with ratios, proportions, and their applications to problems involving work and motion, but these problems are not a main focus at this level
- Radicals, Exponents, and Logarithms: Simplest Radical Form for Roots, Laws of Exponents, Laws of Logarithms including change of base
- Complex Numbers: Arithmetic Operations and writing in rectangular form
- Factoring Tricks: Sums and differences of squares, cubes, etc., Expanding $(x+y)^n$ using Pascal's triangle
- Solving Equations: Linear Equations, Quadratic Equations, Systems of Equations, Substitutions to rewrite higher degree equations as quadratics, Radicals, Absolute Values
- Quadratics: Graphing and Vertex Form, Maxima and Minima, Quadratic Formula, Discriminant

- Polynomials: Polynomial Long Division, Remainder and Factor Theorem, Rational Root Theorem

Geometry

- As a general rule students should be comfortable using algebraic techniques (linear equations, quadratic equations, systems of equations, etc.) as tools for applying the geometric concepts listed below
- Angles in Parallel Lines (corresponding angles, alternating interior/exterior angles, same-side interior/exterior angles, etc.)
- Analytic Geometry: Equations of Lines, Parabolas, and Circles, Distance Formula, Midpoint Formula, Geometric Interpretation of Slope and Angles
- Triangles: Congruence and Similarity, Pythagorean theorem, Ratios of Sides for triangles with angles of 45, 45, 90 or 30, 60, 90
- Trigonometry: General understanding of sine, cosine, tangent, and their cofunctions, Law of Sines and Cosines, Trigonometric Identities for double angles, sums/differences, etc.
- Centers in Triangles: Definitions of altitudes, medians, angle bisectors, perpendicular bisectors
- Interior and Exterior Angles of Polygons, including the sum of all these angles, each angle if the polygon is regular, etc.
- Areas and Perimeters of basic shapes such as triangles, rectangles, parallelograms, trapezoids, and circles, Heron's formula and formulas using inradius or circumradius for triangles
- Geometric Reasoning with Areas: Congruent shapes have the same area, Similar triangles have a ratio of areas that is the square of the ratio of their sides, Triangles with the same height have a ratio of their areas equal to the ratio of their bases, etc., Using multiple expressions of area to solve for unknowns

3.1 Division H Topics Covered

- Circles: Arc Length, Sector Area, Definitions for Tangent Lines and Tangent Circles, Inscribed Angles, Angles formed by intersecting chords
- Solid Geometry: Surface Area and Volume for Spheres, Prisms, Pyramids, and Cones, Reasoning for more general solids, such as combining the solids listed above or pieces of solids when cut by a plane, etc.

Counting and Probability

- Fundamental Rules: Sum and Product Rules, Permutations and Combinations
- Counting Methods: Complementary counting, Grouping objects that must be together, Inserting objects that must be apart into spaces between objects, etc.
- Sequences: Arithmetic and Geometric Sequences and Series, Finding and understanding patterns and recursive definitions for general sequences
- Probability and Sets: Definitions for event, sample space, complement, intersection, and union, Understanding the use of Venn Diagrams
- Probability: In finite sample spaces as a ratio of the number of outcomes, In geometric sample spaces as a ratio of lengths, areas, or volumes, Axioms of Probability, Independence, Conditional Probability, Law of Total Probability

Number Theory

- Fundamental Definitions: Prime numbers, factors/divisors, multiples, least common multiple (LCM), greatest common factor/divisor (GCF or GCD), perfect squares/cubes/etc.
- Divisibility Rules for numbers such as 2, 3, 4, 5, 8, 9, 10, 11, and how to combine the rules for numbers such as 6, 22, etc.

- (Unique) Prime Factorization and how to use the prime factorization to find the number of factors, to test whether a number is a perfect square/cube/etc, to find the LCM or GCD.
- Factoring Tricks: Factors come in pairs, perfect squares have an odd number of factors, etc.
- Remainders: Patterns for finding remainders, for example units digits or last two digits

3.2 Glossary of Common Math Terms

Acute Angle An angle less than $90°$.

Altitude of a Triangle A line segment connecting a vertex of a triangle to the opposite side forming a right angle. Also called the height of a triangle.

Angle A figure formed by two rays sharing a common vertex. Often measured in degrees.

Angle Bisector A line dividing an angle into two equal halves.

Arc The curve of a circle connecting two points.

Area The amount of space a region takes up. Often denoted using square brackets: area of $\triangle ABC = [ABC]$.

Arithmetic Sequence A sequence where the difference between one term and the next is constant.

Average See Mean.

Base of a Triangle One side of a triangle, often used when the altitude is drawn from the opposite side to this base.

Binomial Coefficient The symbol $\binom{n}{k} = \dfrac{n!}{k!(n-k)!}$.

Chord A line segment connecting two points on the outside of a circle.

Circle A round shape consisting of points that all have the same distance (called the radius) from the center of the circle.

Circumference The perimeter of a circle.

Circumscribe To draw a shape outside another shape so that the boundaries touch.

Coefficient The number being multiplied by a variable or power of a variable. For example, the coefficient of x^3 in $5x^5 + 4x^3 + 2x$ is 4.

Complement In probability, the complement of a set is all elements outside the set.

Composite Number A number that is not prime.

Congruent Two shapes or figures that are exactly the same.

Cube A solid figure formed by 6 congruent squares that all meet at right angles.

Deck of Cards A standard deck of cards has 52 cards. There are 4 suits (clubs, diamonds, hearts, and spades) with each suit having cards of 13 ranks (A (ace), $2, 3, \ldots, 10, J$ (jack), Q (queen), and K (king)).

Degree of a Polynomial The highest power of a variable in the polynomial. For example, the degree of $2x^3 - 5x^6 + 2$ is 6.

Denominator The bottom number in a fraction.

Diagonal A line segment connecting two vertices of a shape or solid that is not an edge of the shape or solid.

Diameter A chord passing through the center of a circle. The diameter has length that is twice the radius.

Die or Dice A standard die (plural is dice) has 6 sides. Each of the 6 sides has the same chance when the die is rolled.

3.2 Glossary of Common Math Terms

Digit One of $0, 1, 2, \ldots, 9$ used when writing a number.

Discriminant The expression $b^2 - 4ac$ for a quadratic equation $ax^2 + bx + c = 0$.

Distinguishable Objects Objects that are different.

Divisible A number is divisible by another number if there is no remainder when the first number is divided by the second. For example, 35 is divisible by 7.

Divisor A number that evenly divides another number. For example, 6 is a divisor of 48. Also called a factor.

Edge A line segment connecting two vertices on the outside of a shape or solid.

Equally Likely Having the same chance of occurring.

Equiangular Polygon A shape with all equal angles.

Equilateral Polygon A shape with all equal sides.

Equilateral Triangle A regular triangle, one with three equal sides and three equal angles.

Even Number A number divisible by 2.

Exponent The number another number is raised to for powers. For example, in a to the power of b (a^b), the exponent is b.

Face The shape or polygon on the outside of a solid region.

Factor of a Number A number that evenly divides another number. For example, 6 is a factor of 48. Also called a divisor.

Factorial The symbol ! where $n! = n \times (n-1) \times (n-2) \cdots \times 1$.

Fraction An expression of a quotient. For example, $\frac{1}{2}$ or $\frac{9}{7}$.

Function A function is a rule that associates exactly one output with every input. Often described using an equation.

Geometric Sequence A sequence where the ratio between one term and the next is constant.

Greatest Common Divisor/Factor (GCD/GCF) The largest integer number that is a divisor/factor of two or more numbers.

Indistinguishable Objects Objects that are the same.

Inscribe To draw a shape inside another shape so that the boundaries touch.

Intersecting Lines or curves that cross each other.

Intersection of Two Sets The set of objects that are in both of the two sets. Denoted using $\cap$. For example, $\{2,3\} \cap \{3,4,5\} = \{3\}$.

Isosceles Triangle A triangle with two equal sides and two equal angles.

Least Common Multiple (LCM) The smallest number that is a multiple of two or more numbers.

Mean The sum of the numbers in a list divided by the how many numbers occur in the list. Also called the average.

Median The number in the middle of a list when the list is arranged in increasing order.

Median of a Triangle A line connecting a vertex in a triangle to the midpoint of the opposite side.

3.2 Glossary of Common Math Terms

Midpoint The point in the middle of a line segment.

Mode The number or numbers occurring most often in a list of numbers.

Multiple A number that is an integer times another number. For example, 72 is a multiple of 8.

Numerator The top number in a fraction.

Obtuse Angle An angle between 90° and 180°.

Odd Number A number not divisible by 2.

Parallel Lines Lines that do not intersect.

Perfect Cube A number that is another number cubed. For example, $64 = 4^3$ is a perfect cube.

Perfect Square A number that is another number squared. For example, $64 = 8^2$ is a perfect square.

Perimeter The length/distance around the outside of a shape.

Perpendicular Bisector A line perpendicular to and passing through the midpoint of a line segment.

Pi (π) A number used often in geometry. $\pi = 3.1415926\ldots \approx 3.14 \approx \dfrac{22}{7}$.

Polygon A shape formed by connected line segments.

Polynomial A function that is made of adding multiples of powers of a variable. For example, $f(x) = x^4 + 3x^2 + 2x - 3$.

Prime Factorization The expression of a number as the product of all its prime factors. For example, 24 has prime factorization $2 \times 2 \times 2 \times 3 = 2^3 \times 3$.

Prime Number A number whose only factors are one and itself.

Proportional Ratios Ratios that have equal values when expressed in fraction form. For example, $2:3$ is proportional to $8:12$.

Quadratic A polynomial with degree 2. Often written in the form $ax^2 + bx + c$.

Quadrilateral A shape with four sides.

Quotient The integer quantity when dividing one number by another. For example, the quotient of $38 \div 5$ is 7 as $38 = 7 \times 5 + 3$.

Radius of a Circle The distance from the center of the circle to any point on the outside of the circle.

Randomly Chosen for a group of objects. Unless specified, the chance of choosing each object is the same as any other object.

Rank of a Card See Deck of Cards.

Ratio A relation depicting the relation between two quantities. For example $2:3$ or $\frac{2}{3}$ denotes that for every 3 of the second quantity there are 2 of the first quantity.

Rational Number A number that can be written as a fraction.

Reciprocal One divided by the number. For example, the reciprocal of 7 is $\frac{1}{7}$.

3.2 Glossary of Common Math Terms

Rectangle A quadrilateral with four right angles (an equiangular quadrilateral).

Rectangular Form (of a complex number) A complex number written in the form $a + b \cdot i$ for real numbers a and b.

Regular Polygon A polygon with all equal sides and all equal angles (equilateral and equiangular).

Remainder The quantity left over when one integer is divided by another. For example, the remainder of $38 \div 5$ is 3 as $38 = 7 \times 5 + 3$.

Rhombus A quadrilateral with four equal sides (an equilateral quadrilateral).

Right Angle A $90°$ angle.

Right Triangle A triangle containing a right angle.

Root of a Function A value of x such that the function evaluates to zero. For example, $x = 2$ is a root of the function $f(x) = x^2 - 4$.

Sample Space In probability, the sample space is the set of all outcomes for an experiment.

Scalene Triangle A triangle with three unequal sides and three unequal angles.

Sector The region formed by an arc and the two radii connecting the ends of the arc to the center of the circle.

Sequence An ordered list of numbers.

Set An unordered collection or group of objects without repeated elements. Denoted using curly brackets. For example, $\{1,2,3,4\}$ is the set containing the integers $1,\ldots,4$.

Similar Shapes or solids that have the same angles and sides that share a common ratio.

Simplest Radical Form An expression containing a radical $\sqrt[n]{a}$ such that the radical does not appear in the denominator, and the number a inside the radical is an integer that has no perfect n^{th} power of a prime as a factor.

Sphere A round solid consisting of points that all have the same distance (called the radius) from the center of the sphere.

Square A shape with four equal sides and four equal angles (a regular quadrilateral).

Subset A set of objects that is contained inside a larger set of objects. Denoted using $\subseteq$. For example $\{2,3\} \subseteq \{1,2,3,4\}$.

Suit of a Card See Deck of Cards.

Surface Area The total area of all the faces of a solid.

Tangent Line A line touching a shape or curve at exactly one point.

Trapezoid A quadrilateral with one pair of parallel sides.

Triangle A shape with three sides.

Union of Two Sets The set of objects that are in one or both of the two sets. Denoted using $\cup$. For example, $\{2,3\} \cup \{3,4,5\} = \{2,3,4,5\}$.

3.2 Glossary of Common Math Terms

Venn Diagram A diagram with circles used to understand the relationship between overlapping sets.

Vertex The intersection of line segments, especially the intersection of sides or edges in a shape or solid.

Volume The amount of space a solid region takes up.

With Replacement When choosing objects with replacement, a chosen object is returned to the others allowing it to be chosen more than once.

3.3 ZIML Answers

ZIML October 2018 Division H

Problem 1:	0.5	Problem 11:	12645
Problem 2:	462	Problem 12:	22
Problem 3:	3900	Problem 13:	6
Problem 4:	5	Problem 14:	70
Problem 5:	33	Problem 15:	200000
Problem 6:	5	Problem 16:	112500
Problem 7:	16	Problem 17:	-3
Problem 8:	306	Problem 18:	33
Problem 9:	11	Problem 19:	7
Problem 10:	9.4	Problem 20:	4

3.3 ZIML Answers

ZIML November 2018 Division H

Problem 1:   5

Problem 2:   45

Problem 3:   43

Problem 4:   4

Problem 5:   9

Problem 6:   72

Problem 7:   290.67

Problem 8:   88

Problem 9:   3

Problem 10:   72

Problem 11:   100

Problem 12:   192

Problem 13:   16

Problem 14:   11

Problem 15: -1

Problem 16:   50

Problem 17:   39

Problem 18:   4620

Problem 19:   5

Problem 20:   240

ZIML December 2018 Division H

Problem 1: 10.28

Problem 2: -2

Problem 3: 4

Problem 4: 22

Problem 5: 61

Problem 6: 30

Problem 7: 23

Problem 8: 3

Problem 9: 1500

Problem 10: -4

Problem 11: 11

Problem 12: 29

Problem 13: 2

Problem 14: 71

Problem 15: 77

Problem 16: 4.2

Problem 17: 225

Problem 18: 24

Problem 19: 148

Problem 20: -2

ZIML January 2019 Division H

Problem 1:   26.7

Problem 2:   41580

Problem 3:   73

Problem 4:   3.25

Problem 5:   −4

Problem 6:   35

Problem 7:   3

Problem 8:   10

Problem 9:   28

Problem 10: 5

Problem 11: 100

Problem 12: 94

Problem 13: 241

Problem 14: 258

Problem 15: 13

Problem 16: 8

Problem 17: 14

Problem 18: 6

Problem 19: 71

Problem 20: 330

ZIML February 2019 Division H

Problem 1: 6

Problem 2: 49

Problem 3: 7

Problem 4: 2520

Problem 5: 37.5

Problem 6: 66

Problem 7: 121

Problem 8: 1

Problem 9: 4

Problem 10: 243

Problem 11: 12

Problem 12: 120

Problem 13: 29

Problem 14: 1

Problem 15: -4

Problem 16: 2.7

Problem 17: 24

Problem 18: 3

Problem 19: 810

Problem 20: 13

ZIML March 2019 Division H

Problem 1:   2

Problem 2:   120

Problem 3:   144000

Problem 4:   64

Problem 5:   20

Problem 6:   45

Problem 7:   4.65

Problem 8:   2.8

Problem 9:   43

Problem 10:   4

Problem 11:   28

Problem 12:   381964

Problem 13:   75

Problem 14:   33

Problem 15:   3600

Problem 16: -12

Problem 17:   3

Problem 18:   33

Problem 19:   18

Problem 20:   6

ZIML April 2019 Division H

Problem 1: 10.3

Problem 2: 2

Problem 3: 1

Problem 4: 60

Problem 5: 5

Problem 6: 25920

Problem 7: 21

Problem 8: 315

Problem 9: 144

Problem 10: 1210

Problem 11: 20

Problem 12: 3

Problem 13: 32

Problem 14: 125

Problem 15: 12296

Problem 16: 35

Problem 17: 6603

Problem 18: 7

Problem 19: 48

Problem 20: 11

ZIML May 2019 Division H

Problem 1:   28

Problem 2:   70

Problem 3:   64

Problem 4:   30

Problem 5:   2

Problem 6:   13.5

Problem 7:   14

Problem 8:   729

Problem 9:   11

Problem 10: 13

Problem 11: 1.8

Problem 12: 93420

Problem 13: 5

Problem 14: 110

Problem 15: 12

Problem 16: -120

Problem 17: -28

Problem 18: 1304

Problem 19: 625

Problem 20: 18

ZIML June 2019 Division H

Problem 1: 102

Problem 2: 25200

Problem 3: 48

Problem 4: 2

Problem 5: 270

Problem 6: 51

Problem 7: 7

Problem 8: 200

Problem 9: 26

Problem 10: 72

Problem 11: 33

Problem 12: 31

Problem 13: 0.7

Problem 14: 84000

Problem 15: 13

Problem 16: 4.2

Problem 17: 66

Problem 18: 1.7

Problem 19: 14.25

Problem 20: 8

www.ingramcontent.com/pod-product-compliance
Lightning Source LLC
Chambersburg PA
CBHW071158160426
43196CB00011B/2125